THE CALGARY HERALD'S

TALES OF THE OLD TOWN

by Leishman McNeill

1867 | 1967

"Tales of the Old Town", by Leishman McNeill, was originally written for The Calgary Herald in 1950 and appeared in the pages of The Herald as a regular feature during Calgary's 75th anniversary year. It was republished as a booklet, and about 25,000 copies were distributed, mostly to schools.

It has been reprinted as one of The Calgary Herald's Centenary projects to meet a demand over the years for a history of Calgary. The original text has been retained, with a few changes to bring it up to date, but the reader should remember that Mr. McNeill wrote "The Tales of the Old Town" in 1950. The order of the chapters has been changed to give the booklet greater continuity of subject matter, and another chapter has been added to give readers (especially school students) a brief but complete history of Calgary from its earliest days to the present.

The Calgary Herald acknowledges with thanks permission by Glenbow Foundation for the use of most of the pictures in this edition; also The Herald is grateful to Mrs. Leishman McNeill for her interest and help. The Herald is happy to reprint "Tales of the Old Town" for a Centenary tribute to the old timers.

COVER PICTURE:

This painting by Bill Brownridge of Calgary is based upon a Glenbow Foundation photograph of Fort Calgary, believed to have been taken in 1878. It shows a group of Blood Indians sitting outside the palisades of the NWMP fort. Others in the picture include - left to right: Constable R. W. Fletcher; Constable T. Christie (on horse); Sam Livingston, leaning on fort wall; Inspector Sir Cecil Denny (seated on chair); Joe Butlin (standing in wagon); Sgt. James Barwis (seated with Indians).

PRICE: $1

THE AUTHOR
Leishman
McNeill

Leishman McNeill, the author of "Tales of the Old Town", was born in Calgary in 1896 and himself epitomized in his lifetime those hardy, self-reliant pioneers of Calgary whose histories and exploits he loved to record.

He was a founder member of the Southern Alberta Old Timers Association, and its honorary secretary from 1943 until his death on Sept. 18, 1964.

He knew most of the old timers personally, grew up with their sons and daughters, and literally knew every street and building in "the old town". "Personally," he wrote, "my earliest recollection of Calgary was a town of 5,000, extending from East Calgary to 2nd St. W., from the Bow to about 14th Ave. . . . St. Mary's (Cathedral) was well out of town . . ."

His uncle, George Frazer, came to Calgary in 1884 and his father, J. C. McNeill, in 1886, and he lived all his 68 years in Calgary.

With his roots deep in Calgary history, he distinguished himself in many ways, one of the most notable being as an expert in federal, provincial and civic electoral procedures. He was one of the few men to serve the federal Conservative and Liberal governments and the provincial Social Credit government as returning officer in Calgary elections.

He was also a life-long friend of the Indians, being honored by them in 1955 when they appointed him an honorary chieftain.

His Honor Grant MacEwan, now Alberta's lieutenant-governor and a noted Western historian, and mayor of Calgary at the time of Mr. McNeill's death, said this about the author of "Tales of the Old Town": "He was a great citizen with a fine sense of humor and an equally fine sense of responsibility. Few men have left behind them a finer record of public service . . . Through his links with the Old Timers Association he was held in the highest esteem throughout Alberta."

CONTENTS

(Index of pictures on page 102)

Commissioner James F. Macleod

CHAPTER 1

The Red Coats Arrive

Just 92 years ago a detachment of NWMP built an unnamed fort on the banks of the Bow and Elbow Rivers. To the south was Fort Macleod; on the St. Mary River stood Fort Whoop-Up. To the west where Morley now stands Rev. John McDougall camped with the Stony Indians. To the east in what was known as the Blackfoot Nation Rev. Albert Lacombe and Father Leon Doucet lived among the Blackfoot.

A Fort built in 1799 stood at Rocky Mountain House, and farther north on the Saskatchewan River stood Fort Edmonton.

Early buffalo hunters and Indians had slaughtered animals by the thousands. Whisky traders were playing havoc with the Indians. The country was wild and lawless, so much so that the government at Ottawa, under Sir John A. Macdonald by act of parliament in 1873 formed a military unit, which became the world-famous North West Mounted Police.

In 1875 a detachment of Mounted Police stood on what is known as the present North Hill and overlooked the valley of the Bow and Elbow.

The North West Mounted Police left Toronto in June 1874. That was an amazing journey when you think of it today — 216 men and 244 horses left Toronto by train to Fargo, North Dakota, and then trekked more than 1,000 miles across the prairies. They must have made an impressive sight when they set off with their bull teams, Red River carts, their horses and cattle.

One of the interesting things to me is the fact that the horses of each troop were of a distinct color — "A" Troop had dark bays, "B" Troop, brown; "C" chestnut; "D" dark grays and buckskins, "E" Troop black, and "F" Troop light bays.

From the start the Mounted Police were dressed in the scarlet tunic. Then they must have been a bit different from the bedraggled weary, half-starved bunch that first saw the Rockies when they reached Sweet Grass Hills three months later — a journey today which in a plane would be a matter of two or three hours — but what an ordeal for them. A thousand miles of riding, tramping and driving, often short of rations and still worse, short of water.

In 1875 Troop "F" was sent north from Macleod to establish a fort where our present city now stands. As a fort or trading centre, Calgary in those days didn't mean very much. The route that the traders and fur-trappers used was overland from Winnipeg to Edmonton, down to Rocky Mountain House, and from there to Bow Fort, west of Calgary. At the coming of the Mounted Police, Fort Walsh and Fort Macleod were the principal trading positions. The fact is that after 1875 the Mounted Police fort at Calgary at one time had been practically abandoned, there being for sometime only one man left in charge here.

It was the coming of the CPR in 1883 that was really the start of Calgary.

CHAPTER 2

How Calgary Was Christened

The naming of Calgary was important in the history of this city, and one cannot describe the event better than by quoting from official correspondence between Ottawa and the Mounted Police written at the time of the arrival in Calgary of that famous force.

Fort Macleod,
29 Feb., 1876

To:
Deputy Minister of Justice,
Ottawa, Canada.
Sir:

As we have now a post or fort at Bow River, it would be as well if it were known by some name. I visited the post about a fortnight ago with Colonel Macleod, and when I was there Inspector Brisebois (who is in command of the station) issued an order without consulting either Colonel Macleod or myself stating that all public documents sent from his fort were to be headed "Fort Brisebois". I, of course, cancelled the order at once, as in the first place Inspector Brisebois had no authority to issue such an order and in the second place the fort was not built by Inspector Brisebois or his troop, and neither the troop nor the people about there wished the place called Brisebois. Colonel Macleod has suggested the name of Calgary, which I believe is "Scotch" for "Clear Running Water", a very

appropriate name I think. Should the minister be pleased to approve of this name I will issue an order to that effect. I have the honour, to be Sir, Your Obedient Servant,
A. G. IRVINE,
Assistant Commissioner.

Reply:

1876

Department of Justice of the Mounted Police:

Assistant Commissioner reports a new post at Bow River which Inspector Brisebois had ordered to be called "Fort Brisebois." This order as of this communication cancelled, and now suggest it be called Calgary, a name suggested by Stipendiary Magistrate Macleod, March 25.

———

James F. Macleod, the colonel mentioned, and after whom the town of Macleod is named, was the father of Mrs. A. E. Cross, Norman T. Macleod, Mrs. George Sharp of Toronto and Mrs. Cecil Townshend, Mrs. J. Montgomerie Bell of Calgary. Col. Macleod is credited as being the man who did so much to bring friendship and understanding between the whites and the Blackfoot Indians, and it is chiefly due to his work with Crowfoot, chief of the Blackfoot Indians, that the Blackfoot remained loyal at the time of the Riel Rebellion, 1885.

Calgary was established in 1875 by F Troop, NWMP, here shown lined up at the fort in 1876.

CHAPTER 3

Whisky Traders

When that pioneer force of 216 members of scarlet-coated North West Mounted Police who had left Toronto in June of 1874 to travel to Fargo, North Dakota, by train and then marched 1,000 miles over the prairies, reached Fort Whoop-Up on Oct. 9, they found it abandoned except for a couple of men. Evidently the whisky traders had heard that they were on their way.

The force first built, with the help of I. G. Baker Company, their first encampment at Macleod, and spent the winter of '74 hunting the scattered whisky traders.

The administration of justice was a bit haphazard in those days. There is a story about one whisky trader who had been caught and had his property of 1,000 buffalo robes confiscated. He got mad and said, "Say, Colonel, is that the law?", and was told that "as matters stand at the present we make the law as we go along."

This was Fort Calgary in 1881, looking north to the Bow River bluffs, with the Elbow, right foreground.

CHAPTER 4
"Peaches" Davis

Before the coming of the Mounted Police in 1875, whisky traders had made the Calgary district a lawless country. Their influence on the Indians was bad and the situation was fast becoming out of control, but with the coming of the Mounted Police law and order was soon established.

Even before the Mounted Police arrived, Forts Whoop-Up, Stand-Off, and Slide-Out were practically deserted.

Every child in school knows the story of the Mounted Policeman, Peaches Davis, the lone Mountie who was sent to Montana and brought back, single-handed, a renegade band of Indians. Such was the fear of British law and justice, as symbolized by the Red Coats of the Mounted Police.

In Calgary's early days there were no gun-toting cowboys; no saloons in this city were ever "shot-up". Of course, there was crime, even as we have it today, but this country was never, after the coming of the Mounted Police, terrifying and lawless.

The saying that is often heard, "The latch string is always out," was a reality in the early history of this district.

Actually the saying came from the fact that many doors were fastened with an inside latch which could be released from the outside by pulling a string attached to the inside lock and passed through a hole to the outside.

Ex-mayor Rider Davis of Macleod, well-known pioneer son and old timer of that district, was kind enough to supply me with the details of the actual building of

Constable "Peaches" Davis

the fort at Calgary.

In 1875 Rider Davis' father, D. W. Davis, was in charge of the I. G. Baker Company's men who built the fort for the Mounted Police.

The first building was made out of dry pine logs 14 feet long. These logs were obtained about six miles up the Elbow River and brought down by boom to the junction of the Bow and Elbow rivers. It did not take the I. G. Baker men long to put up a log building capable of accommodating about 50 men, and stables for about the same number of horses.

Lumber for the doors and flooring was cut with a whip saw by half-breeds, some of whom had been living in the district. Surrounding the buildings was built a log stockade about 10 feet high.

In addition to the fort, the I. G. Baker Company, under Mr. Davis' direction, put up a good substantial store and a couple of dwelling houses, and before long had the store stocked with an assortment of goods of all kinds brought from Fort Benton, and open for business as a trading centre.

At the same time, the Hudson's Bay Company was busy putting up a small log building and soon afterward opened up a trading centre.

Later, the Hudson's Bay Company bought out the I. G. Baker Company. The I. G. Baker Company was an American company that had come in with the fur traders from Fort Benton.

CHAPTER 5

Early Churchmen

Early Western Canadian history reads no differently from the history of other countries. We find among the early pioneers the men of the church. As early as September, 1840, Rev. Robert Rundle, the pioneer missionary, reached Edmonton House. From there he went to Rocky Mountain House, arriving there Feb. 22, 1841.

J. E. Harriott was in charge of the Hudson's Bay post at that point. In April, 1841, Mr. Rundle camped at the foot of Cascade Mountain in Banff for over a month. Rundle Mountain, as everyone knows, was named in honor of this missionary trek.

In Sept., 1845, Rev. Father P. J. de Smet, a Belgian priest, reached the Bow River. From there he went to Rocky Mountain House and stayed in that district until 1846.

It was the churchmen of the 50s to 80s who have written glorious pages in Calgary's history. Rev. Father Albert Lacombe came to Fort Edmonton in 1852. He, and later his assistant, Father Leon Joseph Doucet, worked with the Blackfoot Indians. His mission field extended from his hermitage at Pincher Creek to St. Albert, a few miles north of Edmonton, a distance of 300 miles. The Indians called him by an Indian name meaning "Noble Soul."

Later a terrible epidemic of scarlet fever broke out among the Blackfoot. Hundreds were dying like flies, and they begged "Noble Soul" to come to their camp to help them. Father Lacombe nursed and comforted them until he himself was stricken with the disease, and had to be nursed back to health by his true and ever faithful helper Alexis, a half-breed servant.

The Blackfoot after this epidemic called him "The Man With The Good Heart."

When Father Lacombe heard that the railway was coming across Canada he realized that the Indians would have to be prepared for civilization and the stream of settlers which would follow, and he had to beg his friends in the East for money to start schools and teachers for the Indians. The Indians didn't take very kindly to the railway at first. Some of the young men tore up the track which crossed their lands and there might have been a lot more trouble but for Father Lacombe.

He gave them his word that they would be compensated, and he was one of the first white men they would trust.

When the first train reached Calgary, Father Lacombe was invited into the directors' car for lunch. The president, George Stephen, gave him his chair, and made Father Lacombe president of the CPR for a few hours.

When the CPR built the Calgary-Edmonton railway in 1890 Sir William Van Horne, the president, asked Father Lacombe to suggest the names of the towns between Red Deer and Edmonton.

The names as submitted by Father Lacombe were accepted,

Sir William also personally honored Father Lacombe by including the name Lacombe as the name of one of the principal locations.

Father Lacombe lived until he was 89 and his body is entombed in the shrine at St. Albert.

Father Lacombe

Father Lacombe actually came to the territory now known as Alberta in 1852. He came overland from Fort Garry to establish his mission at St. Albert, near Edmonton. His early missionary work was chiefly among the Cree Indians but his later days were spent among the Blackfoot Confederation in Southern Alberta.

After Fort Calgary was established, Father Doucet took up squatter's rights on what is now known as the Mission district of Calgary and Father Lacombe joined him there.

When Father Lacombe realized that the railway was coming to Calgary in 1883, he went to Ottawa to obtain homesteader's rights on his land which, by this time, had been surveyed. Father Lacombe's visit to Ottawa is recorded by Katherine Hughes in her book "Biography of Father Lacombe" published in 1914.

To quote Miss Hughes:
"Sir David MacPherson was minister of the interior then. One morning as he sat in his office, shut off from the commonplace world by noiseless baize doors and the imposing long Gothic corridors — a priest in a dusty black cassock was ushered in to him.

Father Lacombe

"The plainsman laid his case before the minister. It sounded reasonable. Sir David felt inclined to comply. But the dignity of governments must be upheld — delays and red-tape being the traditional safeguards. Father Lacombe was informed that his request would receive most favorable consideration, and if he returned in a few days he would receive definite confirmation of this.

"That did not meet Father Lacombe's wishes at all. Each day that passed meant more likelihood of newcomers building on his land —and the piling up of abuse or inconvenience for poor timid Father Doucet — 'God's Lamb.'

"His next statement, blandly made, took away Sir David's breath: 'No, Monsieur, I cannot go until I receive that settlement of our land. I came hundreds of miles to you just for this. I will wait here with your permission. I am used to camping on the prairie, on the floor, anywhere — I will just camp here until I get my papers.'

"He looked about him. After the mud-chinked shack at Macleod, or the shedlike house in Calgary, this office was regal. He seated himself with an air of one who settles himself comfortably for a length of time.

"Sir David immediately wrote out a guarantee of the homestead locations on the sections indicated by Father Lacombe. The patents for the land were to follow when the conditions were fulfilled."

Pioneer Protestant Clergy

In the old days, among that notable band of missionaries who did such a splendid pioneering service in the Calgary district were the McDougalls, who were Methodists.

Rev. George McDougall came to Edmonton with his sons in 1865. Unfortunately he was frozen to death in a blizzard near Calgary in the 70s. His son, Rev. John McDougall, founded the first Protestant church in the Calgary district, this being a little church on the highway near Morley.

Rev. John McDougall, like Father Lacombe, went through some hard times in this country. He lost his daughter, in a smallpox epidemic, and he himself was stricken with the disease, but fortunately survived that illness.

He died in Calgary in 1917 within a month of his old friend Father Lacombe.

The Presbyterian Church was represented by Rev. James Robertson and his brother, Rev. Angus Robertson. Rev. Angus founded Knox Presbyterian Church in Calgary in 1883, but unfortunately

Archdeacon J. W. Tims

died as a young man in 1890. Rev. James did missionary work west of the Great Lakes from 1881 to 1902.

The Anglican Church in Calgary was represented by Ven. Archdeacon J. W. Tims, who as a young man came out from Staines, England, under Rt. Rev. W. Cyprian Pinkham, who at that time lived in Winnipeg.

From 1883 to 1895 Mr. Tims was on the Blackfoot Reserve at Old Sun's camp near Gleichen.

Archdeacon Tims was the first Anglican to hold services in Calgary, the father of the Cathedral Church (of the Redeemer) as we now know it.

Rt. Rev. Cyprian Pinkham came to the Red River settlement September 11, 1868, and later to Calgary as bishop of this diocese in 1887.

In 1895 Archdeacon Tims exchanged parishes with Canon H. W. Stocken, who was at that time Anglican minister on the Sarcee Reserve, south of this city.

CHAPTER 6

Chief Crowfoot

Through Fred M. George, a well-known pioneer's son, whose father, Dr. Henry George, was the Mounted Police doctor in the early days, I have been supplied with a newspaper clipping, published in The Calgary Herald in 1890, which describes the death of Crowfoot.

To quote: "Crowfoot, Chief of the Blackfoot, the most important and ablest of all Indian chiefs, died at his home on Friday, April 25, 1890. The Indians, believing on Thursday that he was dead, shot his best horse, according to their custom, but the old warrior revived and lived another 24 hours.

"He died sitting propped up with pillows and blankets, dressed in his finest toggery with beaded tunic, buffalo skin britches and all his grandest clothing, the crow's head of his chieftainship resting on his head, a plume in his right hand, and a pipe in his mouth.

"Three of his wives squatted near him, and around him were a .dozen of the greatest medicine men of the tribe and some 30 other leading Indians.

"Crowfoot requested that his own war song, composed by himself after his first great battle, be sung continuously. He also wore his government hat with gold band and the gold rose.

"For five days and nights, the tom-toms were beating loud enough to be heard six or seven miles away, and the noise and excitement attending a great chief's death had been maintained all that time.

"At the telegraphed request of Minister Dewdney, Dr. Henry George remained until the end, spending from Monday until Friday on the reserve.

"Crowfoot died requesting his people to be good children and remain friendly with the whites. To his brother he gave three bulls, all his cows and all his medals except one — this went to his favorite squaw, who received the Treaty Medal of 1877.

"Crowfoot was buried on Saturday in a grave on the highest ground at the reserve at the Old Blackfoot Crossing. The old man was laid out in state by the side of the grave, dressed up gorgeously, and the usual Indian ceremonial was conducted with all the cries, howling and other noises of excitement.

"The body was placed in a coffin and buried in the ground. At the conclusion of the Indian ceremonies, Father Doucet conducted a funeral service to the forms of the Roman Catholic Church, much to the gratification of the Blackfoot who regarded it as a mark of honor to their deceased chief.

"The old chief seemed to have passed on with becoming dignity — the dignity that was characteristic of his life."

Chief Crowfoot

CHAPTER 7
Pioneer Women

To the pioneer women of Calgary all honor should be given. To them is owed a debt that cannot be measured in words.

Let me sketch briefly the experiences of just three pioneer women, Mrs. David McDougall, Mrs. John McDougall and Mrs. James F. Macleod.

David McDougall first came to this country in 1865. For many years he was chief of the ox-cart brigade of the Hudson's Bay Company's ox-cart transport between Fort Garry (Winnipeg) and Fort Edmonton.

Mrs. David McDougall

In 1871, as a bride, Mrs. McDougall accompanied her husband on one of these hazardous trips, enduring all the trials and hardships of such a journey. Her honeymoon—960 miles in an ox-cart across unchartered prairie inhabited by warring Indians.

Mrs. John McDougall spent the winter of 1872-73 at a little log mission at Morley, at that time the only white woman between the United States boundary and the Saskatchewan River.

Mrs. Macleod, wife of Colonel James F. Macleod, spent her honeymoon trip in the 70s traveling by dog-team from Portage La Prairie to Swan River barracks (Northern Manitoba). Incidentally, Norman Macleod, a well-known Calgary citizen and the son of Col. and Mrs. Macleod, recalls that during the year following that eventful trip, the driver of the dog-team was hanged for a murder he had committed.

Many of the pioneer families came here before the railway in 1883. How did they come? There was only one way — overland; some coming from Fort Benton, Montana, by the Missouri River, and from there by ox-cart to Calgary; others coming overland from Fort Garry to Edmonton.

All experienced hardships unknown today, but they always came through with a smile, living to see their families established and this West of ours settled.

Contrast the life of the pioneer woman with that of the modern girl today—the modern bride, for example, who steps into a car and in three or four days is honeymooning in California; or climbs into a plane to land in London or Paris within a matter of hours.

Many of the early settlements can be attributed to the enterprise of the women pioneers. It was they who made the social gatherings so helpful to the small community. It was they who supported the establishing of centres of worship, of schools and, above all, who gave the encouragement so necessary to their men folk to carry on — for the establishment of homes and the future.

CHAPTER 8

Steele's Scouts, 1885

The year is 1885. George, a boy of 12, is standing, along with many youngsters, on the south bank of the Bow River alongside the ferry.

The boys watched as a company of soldiers gathered on the north shore. Soon George and his friends realized that it was the Sam Steele Scouts returning to Calgary after being away all summer engaged in their fight against the half-breed Louis Riel and his rebels. George and his friends had good reason to know the Steele Scouts. Most of them were local cowboys, whom Sam Steele had recruited that same year in Calgary.

George well remembered the day that the call came for the cowboys in the district to join up. Times were hard and adventure called. Each man who volunteered was required to supply his own horse—for which he was well paid.

The boys were anxious to get across the river to see the Scouts, but George Hamilton, the ferryman, kept chasing them off the ferry. Young George—more venturesome than the rest—jumped on the ferry just as it was backing out. George Hamilton growled at him but let him go across.

Among the Steele Scouts, George saw his friends, Joe Butlin, George Scott and Malcolm McKeller, who said to him, "Go back on the ferry, George, and up to G. C. King's store and bring us our mail."

So back across on the ferry George went—up to G. C. King's store on the corner of 8th Ave. and 1st St. E. When George told Mr. King what he wanted, G.C. gave him two heavy bags of mail. Back went young George to the river, and, when the ferryman wasn't looking, George hid in a wagon that was already on the ferry. George delivered the mail to the Steele Scouts. The cowboys, glad to receive letters months old, accumulated enough silver to give George the unheard of sum of $11. For the rest of the week George was the wealthiest boy in town.

Who's George? George was one of our well known and beloved old timers, George Henderson, the grand secretary of the IOOF for Alberta.

Calgary was famous for many things in the early days, but there was one thing she didn't have, and that was a steamboat. Medicine Hat was the "harbor city" of the plains. Medicine Hat's last and most famous boat was "The City of Medicine Hat." This boat was built and captained by Horatio Ross, a brother of Major George Ross of polo fame who lived in Calgary in the early days.

The boat was built in the winter of 1907-08 in Medicine Hat and was put into service as a pleasure boat between Medicine Hat and forks of the Bow and Belly Rivers. This boat came to a sad ending at Saskatoon during the floods of 1909. It was a high class sternwheeler and was a most unusual sight on the South Saskatchewan River, especially at night with all lights ablaze.

CHAPTER 9

Tall Tales

About 30 years ago it was my privilege and pleasure to know David M. McDougall, who came to the West in 1865. He spent his early years as a transport man between Winnipeg and Edmonton in charge of the Hudson's Bay ox-cart brigade. In 1871 he located at Morley as a fur trader and merchant rancher; and still later set up a building business in Calgary where he erected many prominent buildings.

Many an hour I spent with David McDougall—I loved to hear him tell of his early life; of the hardships of those early days; of the courage of the pioneer women; of long weary trips by Red River carts; of whisky traders; of tough hombres.

Mr. McDougall had a marvelous sense of humor, and let there be someone present who didn't know the West—somebody from the East or the Old Country—and Dave would let fly with both barrels.

Here's one story he'd tell and then slyly look at you and wink. "One cold winter day—about 40 degrees below zero—we were coming in from Morley in a bob-sleigh wrapped in buffalo robes, hot bricks at our feet, fur coats on our backs. The north wind was blowing a howling gale, the coyotes' mournful wail crying in the distance.

"As we came along where Cochrane is now, suddenly the wind changed. In a matter of moments a Chinook was blowing out of the west—the temperature shot up and up. We threw off our buffalo robes, then our coats. The snow-packed, icy road started to melt;

and we knew we had to get to Calgary before the chinook winds melted the road in front of us.

"So—what did I do? I stood up—whipped the horses until they were on the dead run, and would you believe it, for 25 miles we raced the Chinook into Calgary—the front bobs in the snow, the back bobs kicking up the dust behind us. Boys—we just made it."

Another yarn Dave would tell the "foreigners":

"Once when I was out buffalo hunting, I saw in the distance a great herd charging across the prairies, coming right at me. I rode my cow pony at full gallop, trying to get out of range, for I knew that if I were caught in that wild stampede I'd be a goner. I just about cleared the surging mass, but unfortunately my pony tripped in a badger hole and threw me.

"There I was, the surging buffalo upon me. I had no time to get my horse. I thought I was done for; but luck was with me.

"What did I do? I was young and strong. As the surging mass approached, I gave a mighty leap —landing on the broad back of the first animal. The buffalo were so thick, so closely packed together, that I ran across the backs of that mighty herd, leaping from animal to animal until I reached the rim of the herd, whistled for my cow pony, and rode home."

Then Dave would laugh. He knew there were no tremendous herds of buffalo even in his day; just a few scattered animals. But Dave had a great sense of humor that never left him as long as he lived.

CHAPTER 10

The Old Town

1881: Shacks and Teepees

An old timer by the name of Frank White wrote in his diary that in 1881 he stood on Calgary's North Hill and counted 16 log shacks, nine Indian teepees and the Mounted Police fort.

Personally my earliest recollection of Calgary was of a town of 5,000 extending from East Calgary to 2nd Street West from the river to about 14th Avenue. St. Mary's Church on 18th Avenue and the Holy Cross Hospital were well out of town, and when Sir James Lougheed built his home on 13th Avenue (the present Red Cross House) that was just out in the country, that's all.

In Calgary's early history the streets and avenues were named.

Calgary, unlike other towns, didn't have a "Main Sreet." The old timers possibly were more romantic. They called 8th Avenue "Stephen Avenue" in honor of Lord Mount Stephen, president of the CPR. The names of the avenues in my early youth were as follows:

Abbott was 2nd Avenue. Egan was 3rd Avenue. Reinach was 4th Avenue. Northcote was 5th Avenue. Angus was 6th Avenue. McIntyre was 7th Avenue. Stephen was 8th Avenue. Atlantic was 9th Avenue. Pacific was 10th Avenue. Smith was 11th Avenue. Van Horne was 12th Avenue. Kennedy was 13th. Grenfell was 14th. Rose was 15th. Notre Dame was 17th Avenue.

Boynton Hall (centre) on 8th (Stephen) Ave., about 1884-1885.

Indians with travois on 8th (Stephen) Ave., about 1887.

For the streets: McTavish was the present Centre; Scarth was 1st St. W.; Hamilton 2nd St. W.; Barclay 3rd Street West; Ross, 4th Street West; and to the east, Osler was 1st St. East; and here's the best one of all, the street they put the police station and town hall on was "Drinkwater", 2nd Street East; Hardisty was 3rd St. East; Dewdney, 4th St. East; Irvine, 5th St. East; and in East Calgary, Conrad St. was the present 7th St. East.

In recalling these names it occurs to me that as our present city is developing and the city officials will be opening up new sub-divisions, now would be the time to honor the early pioneers by again using these original names, many of which were in honor of CPR officials, prominent Calgarians of that day, and officers of the Mounted Police.

In the small area encompassed in the list of street and avenue names above were built Calgary's early buildings, many of them landmarks until the present day.

Two of the most famous trails leading into the city today are still carrying the names given them by the old timer. The south road is known as the Macleod Trail — over which the supplies came by bull team from Macleod to the little settlement of Calgary. The Edmonton Trail, which connected the two settlements, still carries the name used by the old timer.

14

The Sandstone City

Practically all the early buildings in Calgary were built of sandstone. In the '90s steel and cement were still unheard of here, but the pioneers of Calgary were equal to the occasion. The high hills surrounding this valley are underlined with a superior quality of sandstone which is easily worked and which hardens when exposed to the air.

In the '90s at least 50 per cent of the tradesmen in this town were stone masons.

Imagine what the cost would be in this day and age of a building built of sandstone quarried and cut to size. Stone masons in the '90s received from $1.50 to $2 for a ten-hour day. Carpenters received $1.50 a day. Men working in industries in Calgary in the '90s worked for a monthly wage of from $27 to $30.

But then, of course, we must realize that the cost of living was in proportion to the wages paid.

The sandstone which builders used for foundations and which the stone masons of that day called "rubble", sold for about $6 a cord (128 cubic feet). Dimension sandstone, which was cut to size on the job, sold for approximately $20 a cord.

The first quarries were opened by W. F. Orr in 1886. W. H. Ford, Joe Butlin, J. G. McCallum, William Oliver and Thomas Edworthy (father of a well-known Calgary businessman, George Edworthy) all operated stone quarries at one time or another.

The first building of any size built of sandstone was Knox Presbyterian Church which stood on the present location of the York Hotel.

As early as 1890, the sandstone quarries had an export business, shipping sandstone as far east as Brandon.

Early churches and hospitals - left to right, top: Anglican, and Roman Catholic Cathedrals; centre: General Hospital, First Baptist Church, and Holy Cross Hospital; bottom: Methodist and Presbyterian Churches.

A Romantic Mile

In 1902 all the City of Calgary was contained in an area of less the one square mile. The distance between the Mounted Police barracks on 6th St. E. and the Court House on 4th St. W. was one mile. In that romantic mile Calgary was born and throughout its youth lived a life of hardship, intense excitement, boom and busts, laughter and sorrow. But the old pioneer spirit came through and left us a heritage of which we are justly proud today, "the good old Calgary spirit."

Let us go back to 1902 and take a walk down what is now 8th Ave.—at that time called Stephen Ave.

Then we will go along the avenues that are now called 7th, 8th and 9th Aves., and then over to 6th and 10th Aves., and see them as they were in 1902.

Firstly, let us walk down 8th Ave.

West of 2nd St. W., there were only nine houses. Where Eaton's of Canada store is today there was only open prairie where the Sarcee Indians formed a camping ground when they came to town. The corner where the Royal Hotel stands today was the site of R. C. Thomas's Frontier Stables. Mr. Thomas has often told me how he bought the corner property from William Toole for $1,500, with $500 cash.

The present location of the Canada Life Building was in those days the residence and workshop of William Head the plumber. On the opposite corner, where the Brock Building (Bennett's Restaurant) is today was the residence of H. R. Kitto, who owned a gun and bicycle shop on 1st St. W.

Codville and Co., wholesale grocers, were located between 2nd St. and 1st St. W., and the West Ward primary school had a one-room building located about where the Palace Theatre stands today.

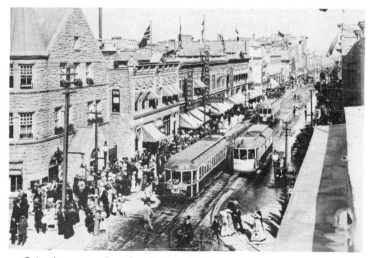

8th Ave. at 1st St. S.W., looking northeast, 1912.

Between the corners of 2nd St. and 1st St. W., there were four houses, one of which was used as an office by R. C. Thomas, and he resided in another for 12 years. According to Mr. Thomas he paid $5 a month rent for each.

A building near the west end of The Bay, once the site of the Temple Duff Drug Co., was occupied then by a Chinese laundry. There is quite a little history to the Temple Duff Co. Originally they operated as the Oliver Drug, and in 1905 were located in the Alberta Block on the corner of 1st St. W. When they incorporated, many years ago, they obtained a crown charter to do business in many lines; build railways, sell hardware, build steamboats, ranching, sell liquor, etc., as well as dispensing drugs.

On the corner of 1st St. W. in 1902 stood Calgary's most imposing building, the Alexander Corner, a three-storey sandstone building, 100 by 50 feet, built in 1891. It was of "romanesque style", meaning corner turret and all the trimmings. The Molson Bank occupied the corner. W. B. Barwis had his real estate office next door; C. S. Lott was in the Alexander Corner, as were MacKay and Dippie, furriers. Upstairs in the building you would find a well-known Calgary citizen, A. M. "Tony" Grogan.

The large hall was taken over by the Perfection Lodge A.F. and A.M. in 1905, and until 1929 it was the home of masonry of this city—all Calgary Masons were proud of the old Alexander Corner. The lodge rooms were beautifully decorated and furnished.

Stephen Avenue

To continue a sight-seeing stroll in retrospect along old Stephen Avenue as it was in 1902, we find that the original Bank of Montreal building on 1st St. W. was built before 1889-1890. It was a splendid 3-storey sandstone building and cost $50,000. This amount would hardly buy the gold leaf that is on the ceiling of their present building. In 1891 A. D. Braithwaite was the bank manager and was succeeded in 1902 by J. O. Wilgress.

Across the street from the bank stood the famous Alberta Hotel.

Next door to the bank was the publishing house of The Herald. At that time, J. J. Young was the managing director. Upstairs, over The Herald, were the offices of P. J. Nolan, Calgary's well-known early lawyer. Also, there were the offices of Muir and Jephson; J. R. Costigan; J. L. "Deafie" Wilson,

the architect; and A. P. Patrick, who was the original surveyor of the city. Mr. Patrick was a wonderful man and remained in Calgary until April 1948, when he died at the age of 99.

J. F. Glanville and William Robertson had a drygoods and men's furnishings store in the Norman Block. Next door was a store where the Midnapore Woollen Mills sold their product. In 1883, the Shaw family came to Calgary from England. They brought with them a complete woollen mill — set up business at Midnapore — and sold their goods in Calgary.

Kenniburg and Co., piano dealers, were located in the Clarence Block. It was here also that George L. Peet had his first office—which later grew into the Toole Peet and Co. Ltd.

Calgary House, the first hotel in 1883, in East Calgary.

W. H. Manarey and John Irwin operated a grocery and butcher business, and Charlie Traunweiser ran the well-known Hub Cigar Store and billiard room. All of these were in the Clarence Block. The McPherson Fruit Co. operated at the rear of the above named concerns. The Lougheed and Bennett law firm had offices upstairs, as well as Crispin Smith and T. A. Thorburn.

In the Tribune Block, next door to the Clarence Block, Wm. M. Davidson had started publishing a semi-weekly paper—The Albertan.

The Calgary Clothing Co., operated by W. G. Richardson, was located next to The Albertan.

In the Lougheed Block, then on Stephen Ave., L. H. Doll operated his jewellery store, and C. T. Gilbert ran the Alberta Bakery.

The Calgary Hardware Co., operated by A. P. Horseman, was

shortly taken over by Ashdowns.

The Hudson's Bay Company in 1902 occupied the corner where the Royal Bank is today.

It might be interesting to note that many of the blocks I mention were owned by Sir James Lougheed: The Clarence, the Norman, the Lougheed (later named the Edgar in honor of his sons).

Next to the Alberta Hotel the CPR had a telegraph office. Alongside was the Wood and Green grocers. A friend of mine who worked for this firm, Tom Shaw, tells me that they had a nursery for the Indian squaws in the store behind the back counter. The Indian women would strap their papooses to their boards (the way they carried them on their backs), and while they shopped, they would stand the board and baby up against the wall.

A wholesale grocery co., operated by G. F. and J. Galt, was situated next to Wood and Green. Another well-known old timer, J. A. Nolan, ran a grocery business also, and next to him was the Neilson Furniture Co., operated by Hugh Neilson.

George E. Jacques, Calgary's first jeweller, came to Calgary in 1881 and had his first store located where the Calgary Shoe Hospital is today.

The Criterion dining hall was where the Bank of Canada is today. Their menus at that time read something like this: breakfast, 25c; dinner, 25c; supper, 25c. And they were real meals, too!

The Calgary Milling Co., operated a flour mill and retail store on 8th Ave. W. The executive was as follows: I. K. Kerr, president; P. A. Prince, vice-president; F. H. Brown, secretary; and William Carson, the father of Harold R. Carson, was manager. John Irwin and W. H. Manerey ran the retail store. This milling company later became the Robin Hood Flour Mills.

The Laurendeau brothers ran the Calgary Wine and Spirit Co. (I'll tell you about their prices later).

Eneas McCormick, of Riley & McCormick, was located next door to Ellis and Grogan (Tony), whose real estate office was just east of the former Club Cafe.

The Union Bank, under the mangement of T. N. Christie; and the Great West Saddlery, managed by R. J. Hutchings, were on 8th Ave. in 1902 and W. R. Hull was located at the southwest corner of Centre St. and 8th Ave.

The Royal Hotel

The Royal Hotel was one of Calgary's earliest stopping houses. It was built about 1885 and for years was managed by James Reilly. The hotel stood on the same site where the Merchants Bank building was later erected — today the Alberta treasury branch occupies this building.

Jimmy Reilly came west to Winnipeg in 1882. He was quite a fellow. An architect by profession, he designed the plans for a portable house which was used extensively by the CPR during construction of the railway. In 1883, Jimmy Reilly came to Calgary. He was mayor of this city in 1891, and that same year he and D. W. Davis ran in the Dominion election for the one seat in Alberta. It was a famous battle, as every old timer will recall, and D. W. Davis won out with a total of 1,087 votes.

The old Royal Hotel held many memories for my father. He came to Calgary in 1886 when 21 years of age, with his cousin George Monilaws. It was toward evening when they arrived and they put up at the Royal. That evening, the Indians were celebrating; a pow-wow was taking place at the corner. The young men were mighty scared as they watched the Indian braves dancing their weird high-jinks, their bodies naked except for a breach cloth, and painted with bright colors. Wouldn't you have been? They would have willingly turned back to peaceful Ontario that night, but with the coming of a bright morning sunshine, things looked different and they ventured out to find jobs.

But we are getting away from Stephen Ave. E. H. Crick owned a shoe store next door to the Royal Hotel. Alongside was S. C. Vick's, the jeweller (called "watchmaker" in those days). Down the line, Mrs. Stirrett had a fruit and confectionery store and Kennisten and Co. operated a bakery. Ed Doughty had the Palace Meat Market.

The Masonic Hall in 1902 was in the Victoria Block, now the Victoria Hotel. A well-known old timer, E. H. Crandell, had his office in the building. In later years, Mr. Crandell opened a brickyard 10 miles west of the city and the siding is still known as Brickburn.

Calgary even had a cigar factory in 1902 called the Alberta Cigar Factory, operated by N. Bell.

Going east from the Victoria Hotel: J. W. Clarke ran the agency for the Singer Sewing Machine Co.; that well-known old timer John Sharples ran a general store in the old McLean Block. The YMCA had a couple of rooms in the McLean Block.

The Calgary Saddlery, operated by A. Carson and Ike Saunders, was alongside the Wendell McLean drug store. Alex McBride had his McBride Hardware close by. I have a photo of this hardware store which shows a Red River cart standing by the front door. Warden Bros. had a bakery just east of the McBride Hardware. The Wardens had a parrot in the bakery window, and that parrot lived to the age of 50 years, being cared for by Mrs. Hiram Warden.

Bob Burdette ran a tobacco store, and on what is now the corner of 1st St. E. and 8th Ave. (where the George McLeod store was, but not the same building), there was a men's furnishing store managed by Findlay McDonald.

The Post Office

In 1902 the Dominion government's post office was at 205 - 8th Ave. S.E., where the Public Building is now. It was a fine sandstone building housing the post office, customs house, government land office, and inland revenue office. (There were no income taxes or income tax office in 1902.)

In 1913, the powers that be tore down the Calgary Post Office and left a hole in the ground for 18 years. It was not until 1931 that the present building was opened as the Public Building and Post Office (1931-1961). Calgary's Post Office, meanwhile, established temporary quarters in the City Market building across from the City Hall, and later moved to the ground floor of the Lancaster Building and then to The Herald Building.

G. C. King was Calgary's postmaster at that time. He was credited with being the first man who saw the site of Calgary when he came in with the Mounted Police in 1875. After he left the police, he opened his first G. C. King general store on 9th Ave. E. and 5th St. Later he located where the Dominion Bank building is today. For a number of years he ran the post office in connection with his store. He sold out to H. A. Hatfield when a permanent post office was established and he was appointed postmaster.

Next to the post office building, C. A. Wallace ran a drug store; and next to him a well-known Calgary citizen, J. T. McDonald, has his grocery store.

J. G. Van Wort operated a feed store next to J. T. McDonald's grocery, and Henry Hoskins ran a second-hand store next door. Alex and Adam McTavish, blacksmiths and carriage builders, had their shop near the corner of 2nd St. E. W. Pipman ran a grocery store on the corner of 2nd St. E. where the Burns Building is today. The Queen's Hotel, operated by S. J. Clarke (later Commissioner Clarke) was a well-known hotel to all old timers. A steam laundry, operated by W. Lyman & Son, was east of the Queen's Hotel.

East of the barracks, on 6th St. E., there were only 14 houses. Across from the post office in 1902, a well-known old timer, S. A. Ramsay, operated an implement agency; Charlie Ramsay a barber shop; George Banks a tailor shop; and on the corner of 8th Ave. and 2nd St. E., W. J. "Billy" Haliday ran his bakery.

On the northeast corner of 8th Ave. and 2nd St. E., the poor house, of all things, was located. Next came the Pacific Stables operated by Frank Hamilton. There were 20 houses between the stables and the barracks. In one of these houses lived that well-known Calgary cattleman, Frank Collicutt. Mrs. Frank Collicutt is the daughter of Calgary's first mayor, George Murdoch. Mrs. Collicutt told me her mother had the first piano ever brought to this country.

That was 8th Ave. in 1902. What will the next 50 years bring?

Banks and Stores

The Imperial Bank was located in Calgary in 1886. S. Barber was the manager from 1891 to 1902, when he was succeeded by M. Morris.

Next to the Imperial Bank was the Royal shoe store owned by J. A. Palmer. In the same building, the Lineham Block, James Findlay had his drug business. Years later the Findlay Drug was taken over by the Liggett Drug Co., and for a number of years operated under the name of Liggett-Findlay Drug Co. The Robinson and Co. dry goods and millinery, was located next door, operated by G. C. Robinson.

In later years, Mr. Robinson operated the Calgary Dry Goods Co. At one time he operated this business in the present Herald Building on 7th Ave. W.

Binning Bros. operated their dry goods store in the Thompson Block in 1902. In those days, ladies ready-to-wear stores were all called dry goods stores.

In 1902, J. S. Mackie had a book store in the Thompson Block. He is credited with having built the Lancaster Building and the Kresge Block in 1912. George King ran a men's furnishing store immediately east of the Thompson Block, and east of this, N. J. Hoad had a tobacco shop. "Cappy" Smart's undertaking parlor was east of this again. He later moved to 1st St. East, next to the Salvation Army headquarters.

James Linton, one of Calgary's best known old timers, ran his book store in the Linton Block. He was a great little fellow — Jimmy Linton — always a joke for everyone. F. E. Osborne, the stationer, often recalled the years when Jimmy would phone him; it was always the same, "This is Linton of the big book store."

The Bell Telephone Exchange was established in a section of Linton's store. C. A. "Charlie" O'Brien was the manager and Miss Bertha Clark was the operator. Just think of it, one operator was all Calgary needed in those days.

Copas and Emerson operated their grocery in the McMillan Block and Owen H. Bott, the English chemist, had his shop in the same block. An earlier druggist in Calgary was **John Fields.**

William Diamond had the Diamond Clothing Co. in the Barber Block, where the English Shop was located. Charlie Benjamin managed the Diamond Clothing for years.

A. L. Cameron, who later built the Cameron Block, ran a grocery store on the corner of 1st St. E. and 8th Ave.

Seventh Avenue

In Calgary's early history, 7th Avenue was known as McIntyre Ave. The Town Hall in 1902 was located on the site of the present City Hall, and was a singular looking wooden structure having height without width. In it were housed the police office and the town prison on the main floor. (I remember well how Chief English and his friends used to sit outside, in bar-room armchairs propped up against the wall.)

Upstairs was the town clerk's office occupied by Charlie McMillan. It was there the council met. Thomas Underwood was the mayor that year.

East of City Hall there were only two houses on McIntyre Ave. The Church of England stood where it is today. Dean E. C. Paget was the rector.

The Salvation Army came to Calgary in August 1887 when Capt. James Desson arrived. A barracks was built on 1st St. E. in 1902.

It is remarkable to realize that it was only nine years previous to this that General Booth first organized his followers into the Salvation Army in London, England. In Calgary, Boynton Hall was used for the meetings before their own barracks were completed, and, as today, they held open air meetings opposite the CPR depot. The little frame barracks was removed in 1909 when the present auditorium was erected.

A. J. Smyth's gun shop was on the corner where the Beveridge Building is today, and in the centre of the block was the famous fire hall. Capt. "Cappy" Smart lived next door, just west of the fire hall.

On the present York Hotel corner stood the Presbyterian Church. Rev. J. C. Herdman was the pastor.

Across the street there were only eight houses besides the Calgary Feed and Livery stable.

Between Centre and 1st St. W. on McIntyre Ave., there were five houses. Felix McHugh lived in one, situated about where the Elks building stands.

On the Greyhound Building corner stood the little Baptist Church with Rev. J. W. Litch the pastor.

In the block where Central United Church stands today, there were three houses, and west of that, as far as 8th St. W., there were only four houses.

Dr. J. D. Lafferty had his residence where The Herald Building is today. On the Hudson's Bay parkade stood the Ranchmen's Club.

M. Morris, who was the manager of the Imperial Bank, was president and L. J. Clarke was secretary of the Ranchmen's Club.

There were only eight houses west of the Ranchmen's Club at that time. J. A. Nolan's home was on the corner of 7th St. W.

About 1905, A. M. Terrill's greenhouses were located on the corner of 6th Ave. and 1st St. W., where the Lougheed Building is today. I remember Mr. Terrill saying he paid a "big" price for that property—$2,500. He sold it a few years later at a tremendous profit.

On the opposite corner was the home of George K. Leeson, who was a great character. He and Mr. Scott ran the stage coach line between Macleod and Edmonton before 1890.

The Methodist Church in 1902 was located on 2nd St. W. Rev. Fred Langford was pastor. The building was later taken over by the Arlington Hotel (now site of the Brown Building).

Chinatown, such as it was at that time, was on 1st St. W., between 10th and 11th Avenues.

W. H. Cushing operated his sash and door factory on the corner of 1st St. W. and 12th Ave. Across the street were John Emery's greenhouses.

The homes of Calgarians were located in the area north of 7th Ave. to the river, and south of the railway to 17th Ave. By 1902 many of the fine old homes had been built on 4th Ave. and a few along 1st St. E. and 1st St. W.

We have scanned the town as it was in 1902. You may have noticed there were no theatres mentioned. The Hull Opera House, on 6th Ave. and Centre St., was the one and only theatre so called.

Ninth Avenue

In Calgary the street that so many towns called Railway Street was first known as Atlantic Ave., now 9th Ave. On it were located many of the early hotels and livery stables. Hotelmen of the old days made it easy for the cattlemen, for they invariably were located next door to a livery stable.

In 1902 there were only five houses west of 4th St. W. on Atlantic Ave. The Calgary Milling was located on its property at 4th St. W. and is now the Robin Hood Flour Mill Ltd. plant. R. C. Thomas had a lumber yard along here. The only other building was the Alberta stable, operated by

Johnnie Hamilton, and later the RCMP garage.

On the present site of the Grain Exchange Building there was a Chinese laundry. Ernie King, who came to Calgary as a boy in 1887, told me that a smallpox epidemic broke out in that little laundry about 1902.

Across the street was the Massey-Harris Implement warehouse. J. G. Douglas was the agent, succeeded by that well-known Calgarian, Alfred F. Tuckey. The remodelled building was later the H. L. Perry Block (now site of the Post Office).

The railway subway on 1st St. W. was level in 1902.

The corner where the Palliser Hotel stands today was the location of the CPR immigration office. At that time the CPR property consisted of a sandstone building which housed the station (if you would like to see Calgary's early station, go down to High River and see their station—that's it); the CPR land office, the ticket offices, etc., and Mrs. E. Bowden's CPR dining room. How well I remember, as a boy, seeing Mrs. Bowden out on the platform, ringing the dinner bell advertising a a good meal for a cost of only about 35c. The CPR gardens from 1st St. W. to 1st St. E. were the pride of all early Calgarians, and well they might be, for they were beautifully landscaped and tended.

East of 1st St. E. on Atlantic Ave., on the side of the railway, there were no buildings of any description.

Sarcee Indians on 7th Ave. in 1909. Knox Church and Hull's Opera House in background.

Hotels and Stables

In 1902 the Alberta Hotel sample rooms were located on the corner of 1st St. W. and Atlantic Ave.

Patrick Burns had his office across from the Palliser Hotel—a tiny office that today would not house the Burns Foods Ltd. mailing department.

In the old garage next to P. Burns, W. H. Lee had his blacksmith and carriage building shop. Years ago, when workmen were tearing down a partition, they came across an original wall which still bore the burned imprints of many of the old cattle brands of bygone days.

The Windsor Stables, operated by P. W. Garnet, were located about where the parking lot was. The Windsor Hotel was next and the Palace Hotel was located on its present site and was managed by C. Christonson. The Commercial Hotel, which was located where the Yale beverage room is today, was operated by J. E. Reilly.

W. D. Thornton had his blacksmith shop between Centre St. and

1st St. E. Next was the New Brunswick Hotel. The Grand Central Hotel, operated by Hugh Mc-Leod, was next to the Bain Stables. These stables were run by William M. Parslow, father of a well-known Calgarian, Vern Parslow.

One of Calgary's landmarks, the Bain Stables, was later managed by Johnny Hamilton. Johnny was a real western character who came here from the Cariboo country in B.C. He had been a stage coach driver in the romantic period of the Cariboo Trail. He originally came around the Horn to Vancouver in a sailing vessel and many of his exploits were well advertised by Bob Edwards in his heyday.

Thousands of Calgarians and visitors each year view the famous Calgary Stampede parade. In the old timers section appears Johnny Hamilton's famous old covered hack. The passengers riding in style, enclosed, the poor driver perched high. But then, in Johnny Hamilton's day, the coachman wore a buffalo coat and usually was well fortified from within.

What stories that old hack could tell!

East of 1st St. E., S. G. Van Wort ran a large lumber yard; Scott Bros. had their livery stable; and the Imperial Hotel was on the same location as today and was operated by Joe Charbonneau.

East of 3rd St. E., the Calgary Iron Works were operated by David Suitor. The Atlantic Stables and the Atlantic Hotel were east of there. There were 19 houses from there to the Mounted Police barracks. Mrs. Ralph Bell, who came to Calgary in 1880 with the Mounted Police lived in one of these houses.

I remember being at a Mounted Police veterans' reunion a few years ago when Ralph Bell met a former Mountie he had not seen for 50 years, who began recalling the olden days with "Remember when you ran the ferry across the Bow for the police?"

They were away with stories for the evening—stories that would fill a book

Fortunes Beckon

It is said that if our foresight was as good as our hindsight, we would all be wealthy! How true!

I am going to give a few interesting facts on property values of this city in the early days.

In 1884 the CPR townsite was put on the market. The first man to buy some of this property in the city centre, as we know it today, was John Glenn, who bought the northwest corner of 9th Ave. and Centre St. for $200.

P. Turner Bone bought the lot east of where the Dominion Bank stands today for $300.

For 15 years the CPR sold their township through a company known as the Canadian Pacific Townsite Company. Lots on 9th Ave. between 1st St. W. and 4th St. W. sold for $100 each — 10 per cent cash with payments over a period of four years.

Sir James Lougheed bought 30 lots from the townsite company, paying $200 to $300 per lot. Today the city centre pivots around these sites.

Judge Travis bought lots on 7th Ave. W., and 4th Ave. W. for $10 each.

As late as 1905, Dr. T. H. Blow bought property on 7th Ave. for $200 a lot.

In 1912 the Hudson's Bay Company sold the corner which is now the Royal Bank corner for $400,000. The lots were originally bought from the townsite company.

In 1904 A. A. Dick bought the quarter section known as Mt. Pleasant, extending from 4th St. E. to Centre St. and from the river to 12th Ave. N.E., for $19,000. This property today is worth millions of dollars. Mr. Dick was telling me recently of the time he bought the Parkhill subdivision in 1906 from Dr. N. J. Lindsay. After buying it, he had it surveyed; advertised for one week, and in one day sold the property at a profit of more than $40,000.

Between 1904 and 1914 money was made and lost in Calgary in a hurry. Calgary had a real estate boom — no mistake about that. Ask any old timer what he "could have done."

One true story is about a chap we shall call "Smith", who had the misfortune of suffering a nervous breakdown and was sent to Ponoka for a period. He was later cured and discharged from that institution just about the time of the 1913-1914 oil boom. He owned some property and sold a section of this land for $10 an acre — $1,600. When his lawyer asked him what he was going to do with the money, he said, "I'm going to buy Monarch Oil shares at $1 a share."

"Why man, you are crazy," exclaimed the lawyer, and Smith was quick to reply, "No, I am not crazy. I have a certificate to prove it," at the same time displaying his discharge certificate.

Smith bought the oil shares — the market advanced to $40 a share — he sold out at the peak and retired to the Okanagan to live the life of Riley.

The First Lougheed Home

Thousands of Calgarians will remember Norman Lougheed, who wrote to me as follows about the house of his father, Sir James Lougheed:

"On your journey along 8th Ave. (Stephen Ave.) you overlooked the small house my father built, where the Ashdown's Hardware store now is located. This small house was built about 1884 and was the first house in Calgary with a bay window. My brother Clarence and I were born there."

"Later on the house was moved back to 7th Ave. and my father built a high board fence around it. Inside the fence he kept a horse and a cow. One day during the absence of the family the horse got into the house and did quite a bit of damage to the interior and the furniture. When my mother arrived home, the horse was in the middle of the bedroom.

"This same little house was then moved up to 4th Ave. W. where it is still located. It is the second house west of 4th St. W. on the south side."

In 1892, Norman's father built the magnificent Lougheed residence on 13th Ave. W., and for years, Sir James and Lady Lougheed received and welcomed all royalty and distinguished visitors to the city in the drawing rooms of this mansion which were the centre of all Calgary society gatherings.

A letter from Mrs. R. N. W. Shillington of Kaslo, B.C., refers to the article on the first white baby born in Calgary:

"Two weeks before Miss Costello was born in Calgary (who I called the first white child born in Calgary), another baby girl was born on the site where the cemetery now is, to Mr. and Mrs. Carney, who had a farm just outside the city limits at that time. This lady is now (1950) Mrs. Sarah Shillicorn, living here in Kaslo with her brother, Gussie Carney."

From Mrs. Doris N. Thomlinson of Castlegar, B.C.:

"My father-in-law, H. C. Thomlinson, who lives with us, often speaks to my children a little Indian, which he learned in Calgary in the early days. While there he had various occupations. One was running the hand press that printed The Weekly Herald."

Another from Robert Kenneth of Vancouver:

"We made all our own amusements in the pioneer days. We could get a nice saddle pony from the Sarcees for $15, and a big load of hay for $5. We rode out to the ranches on Sunday and were always invited for dinner. I used to ride to Gleichen on a bicycle and found it a long travois trail over the prairies 56 years ago.

"I attended W. H. Cushing's Bible class, and we had a class of Chinese. In those days they all wore pigtails and Chinese clothes. Miss James taught the class and of course the usual collection was taken up. One Chinese asked why the collection. Miss James replied, "It is for Jesus." The Chinaman replied: "What for Jesus he all the time-e-stone-broke-e?"

It's An Old Story

The other day when looking over an old copy of The Prairie Illustrated, a weekly paper edited by T. B. Braden. Calgary Herald in 1891, I came across a little ditty that I believe all citizens will agree could have been written yesterday.

Here is what the citizens thought of the conditions of the highways on Jan. 24, 1891:
"The Mission Bridge is full of holes,
Yet no one cares a speck,
That some poor horse might break his leg
Or some poor man his neck.
What is the best course to pursue,
It is, we must consider,
Cheaper to mend the bridge at once,
Than compensate the widder."

Bob Edwards wrote in The Eye Opener of July 2, 1904, the following:

"I'm glad I am a child," remarked the infant prodigy as it poked its little head out of the baby carriage and cast a critical glance up Stephen Avenue.

"Why, my darling skookumwookums?" asked the fond mother.

"Because I stand a show of living for 75 years longer and perchance seeing the day when Stephen Avenue will be free from incumbrances in the shape of excavations, gravel heaps, sand mounds, mortar beds, pipes, barricades and street-corner loafers."

"Oh you dear sanguine child!"

Log house, now on St. George's Island and said to be Calgary's first house, 1882.

Homesteaders in the Suburbs

Calgary in 1902 did not cover much territory. That was before the days of Freddy Lowes and the real estate boys. By the time the real estate brokers were finished in 1914, enough land had been subdivided to cover a city the size of Chicago.

In the early days, so the story goes, a well-known rancher decided to sell some ranch land and invest in city property. After being driven some miles out to see the city lots, the real estate man said, "Well, here we are," and proceeded to give the rancher a sales talk on the wonderful buy. "Now, where is the farm you wish to sell?"

"Oh," replied the rancher, "we passed it three miles back."

Once, when I was in Red Deer, an old-timer was telling me that in 1903 he turned down an offer to buy lots in the Mount Royal district because he thought the price too high—$3 a lot.

In imagination, let's take a walk around the city in 1902. We won't have to walk very far. The North Hill was open prairie. "Crockery Eyed Thompson" owned the half-section which is now Crescent Heights, and was later followed by the McArthur family.

The Rt. Rev. Bishop Cyprian Pinkham and his family lived across and to the left of the Langevin Bridge.

Bridgeland consisted of 28 houses.

The Hillhurst district was homesteaded by Thomas Riley and his sons. It was not until 1904 that the Hillhurst district was subdivided and put on the market. When the Hillhurst district was incorporated into the city limits the Riley family generously gave to the citizens the property known today as Riley Park.

J. J. McHugh lived in the Sunnyside district. In 1882 the McHughs took up squatters' rights in this district, but unfortunately they picked a CPR section. Later the

CPR offered them the 640 acres for $3 an acre, but, being a fighting Irishman, J. J. fought them. "Bull" McHugh tells me it cost his father $2,000 to contest the law suit. The CPR finally gave him one acre—as a peace offering. It was on this acre in Sunnyside that J. J. McHugh first lived.

Alfred S. McKay homesteaded the Parkdale district.

The Killarney and South Calgary districts were homesteaded by Charlie Jackson and his brother Tom.

A few sandstone quarries were in operation along 17th Ave. W. and in the Shaganappi district (Shaganappi — an Indian word meaning rawhide). Thomas Edworthy homesteaded and operated a stone quarry along the south banks of the Bow River.

The Nimmons family were located just off 14th St. and 17th Ave. W. The little old white homestead house is still there.

Elbow Park was a racetrack. By the Mission Bridge, "Irish" ran the Blue Rock hotel. My friend Baldy Buck—a cowboy—tells me that when they came to town, the first stop on the way in and the last stop going out was at "Irish's." "Irish" had a popular custom with the cowboys who stayed with him —an "eye opener" on the house every morning.

In 1902, the district south from 17th Ave. (then outside the town limits) was called Rouleauville. Aside from the St. Mary's Chapel and the convent, there were 18 houses.

In the Mission district around the Holy Cross hospital, there were seven homes.

In 1902, the Agricultural Grounds, now the famous Stampede Grounds, were at their present location.

Section 14, East Calgary, consisted of the Calgary Brewery, the CPR, Hull Brothers and Company, the P. Burns Company, the Elbow Ward school and 37 homes.

William Pearce, one of Calgary's early settlers, had his home on the banks of the Bow River.

Col. James Walker, who came to Alberta in 1874 with the original Mounted Police troop, started his home in 1881. During the floods a few years later the home was washed away, and Col. Walker rebuilt the home where his son, Selby Walker, and family resided in the Inglewood bird sanctuary district.

Calgary's centre consisted of one square mile: that romantic mile from the Court House on 4th St. W., to the Mounted Police Barracks on 6th St. E., and from the river south to 17th Ave.

CHAPTER 11

The Alberta Hotel

Speak to an old timer about Calgary's early days and inevitably he will start telling you about the Alberta Hotel.

Situated as it was, and as the building is today, in the centre of town, it was the mecca of all old timers. It would be interesting to

know how many hundreds of pioneers spent their first night under its hospitable roof — to start out the next morning in search of a job; how many Eastern travellers wired head office that business was so good in Calgary that they would have to stay another week;

how many remittance men, fresh from the Old Country, set out to learn the hard way.

Many an Old Country man who arrived in Calgary, accustomed at home to having his shoes shined while he slept, found them the first morning after his arrival, sitting outside his door — shined all right — not with polish, but with whitewash.

The Alberta Hotel was built in 1889 by T. S. C. Lee and Mr. Brayley, and the building still stands in Calgary's business centre, at the southeast corner of 8th Ave. and 1st St. S.W. (the Alberta Corner).

The hotel opened under the management of H. A. Perley — the same Mr. Perley who later willed the city money to build the Perley wing of the General Hospital. The Alberta later was taken over by Norman D. Jackson who operated it until 1908, when Charles Taprell took over. Mr. Taprell operated the Alberta Hotel until he dramatically closed its doors on that eventful day — July 21, 1916 — the day men stopped standing up to drink and women started — PROHIBITION.

The Alberta Hotel, 1893.

Here is the way I remember the the Alberta Hotel. Stone steps led down from Stephen Ave. to the basement to the Alberta Barbershop. Shortly after 9 o'clock, the Stephen and Atlantic Ave. business men would start coming in for their daily shave. Charlie Traunweiser managed the shop. Jack Rose and George Benedict were the barbers who lathered you up and clipped the whiskers while your cronies sat around and talked about Calgary's future. It was not at 10 o'clock coffee as today, but in the barbershop where one found his friends.

The Rotunda upstairs, filled with over-stuffed leather furniture, led off to the most famous bar between Winnipeg and Vancouver. The bar in the hotel was situated where the Picardy store used to be, and extended the depth of the building.

The good-natured humor of the old timer found its zenith there. In Calgary's early history, government officials did not have to worry about mixed drinking. The bartenders did the mixing. No lady would ever have thought of frequenting a bar; pardon me — there was one woman who did — one famous woman in Calgary's early history — Mother Fulham.

Rough and Ready Humor

My friend "Baldy" Buck tells me of the evening he and his friends were standing around in Calgary in the old days and a prominent Calgarian said to him, "Baldy, would you like a drink?" "Baldy," never hesitant, said, "sure!"

"Just follow me and I'll get you one," said the old timer, and with that he went into the long narrow hallway where the patrons hung their overcoats. Putting out both elbows as he walked down the narrow aisle, he soon struck a bottle. "Here you go, Baldy!"

The story is told of the selfsame Calgarian who one evening during the Scott Act period (prohibition) was entertaining in a hotel a well-known Eastern judge. During the evening, the judge remarked he would like a drink. The Calgarian said, "we will get one. I know a 'blind-pig' down the street." And the two went to the house, entering by the kitchen door. To the judge's surprise no one was around, but the Calgarian said, "never mind, I know where he keeps the bottle."

They then proceeded to have a couple. On leaving, the judge said, "how about paying for the drinks?" "Oh," said the Calgarian, "just leave a couple of bucks on the table. He will find it when he comes in." The following evening, on being invited to his friend's home for dinner, the Easterner found he had been there the evening before. You have guessed it — it was the Calgarian's own home.

Just the other day I heard a luncheon speaker, Rev. Dr. Charles Taylor of Pasadena, California, give a wonderful talk. The subject was "Keeping sane in a crazy world." He stressed the need of humor and laughter, the need of not taking oneself too seriously. Early Calgarians may not have had much in the way of professional entertainment, but just to live in Calgary in those days of which I speak was entertainment enough. Everyone was your friend. As long as you were not a stuffed shirt, your life was a happy one.

I remember one story about "Deafie" Wilson. To Calgary in the early days there came an Easterner, in his youth. He was a pompous fellow and always wore a Christie stiff hat. One day he strutted in his usual manner into the Alberta Hotel dining room, looking neither to right nor left, and demanded a table to himself. "Deafie," David McDougall and David Jr. were having their lunch. With the apple pie the hotel served Limburger cheese. Mr. McDougall didn't eat the cheese. "Deafie" said, "Dave, don't you want that cheese?"

"No," replied Dave. As they left the dining room, "Deafie" picked up the cheese and, passing the hat rack he put the cheese in the rim of our friend's Christie stiff. "That will fix him," said "Deafie."

CHAPTER 12
Early Theatres
Hull Opera House

The Hull Opera House, Calgary's one place of amusement in the early days, was located on Centre St. and 6th Ave. (now the York Hotel parking lot). It was the scene of the firemen's annual New Year's ball, and often the Irishmen's dance on March 17.

It was operated in 1904 by W. B. Sherman. Bill Sherman was a great showman. What I remember best about him was the tremendous diamond stickpin and finger ring that he wore. It was as big as a searchlight.

In those days Calgary was well entertained by amateur theatricals and the prices charged in 1905 at the Opera House were: reserved seat, 25c; dress circle, 50c; matinee, 10c.

There were some wonderfully talented Calgarians in the early days. When Mrs. Roland B. Winter, Mrs. E. G. Mason, Patrick J. Nolan, and others, made up their minds to put on entertainment for charity purposes it was excellent. Many excellent stock companies also used to visit our city in those days.

One well-known Calgarian, Ernie Willis (later he started the Willis Billboard Company) first came to Calgary as an actor with a stock company. Mr. Willis became ill in Calgary and was taken to the General Hospital. Calgarians, in their warm-hearted manner, put on a benefit show for him.

In 1905, the Lyric Theatre was built by Sir James Lougheed. The Lyric was located where the Arcade store is today, on 8th Ave. W. Willis and Cosgrove were the lessees.

About 1910 the Pantages circuit vaudeville opened in the Lyric Theatre. Jeff Liddiatt came to Calgary about that time as manager of the Pantages circuit.

As a boy, I remember being late for supper one evening. "Where have you been?" my parents asked. Proudly I produced a pass to the first picture show that was opening in Calgary that evening. I had, along with some pals (Norman Mackie, former manager of the Imperial Bank was one), been delivering handbills. That was in 1907, and the theatre was the Edison Parlor Theatre, Willis and Cosgrove being lessees. The theatre was next door west of the Lyric and advertised "Moving Pictures, Wonderful, Instructive and Amusing. Admission 10c, 15c Evening; 5c, 10c Matinees. Complete change of moving pictures and illustrated songs twice a week."

The first picture house in Calgary was not very pretentious. It was a long narrow store, the "opera" seats were kitchen chairs; the screen was a white sheet. But Calgarians, as elsewhere, flocked to see the marvelous new invention.

Pearl White in "The Train Robbery", Hal Roach in comedies. Remember them? I can hear the young folks say, "Dearie, You're much older than I".

Soon after the Edison Parlor Theatre started the picture show business in Calgary, other film houses began to open in earnest.

There was the Dreamland, The Starland, The Monarch, The Bijou, built where the Dominion Cafe operates today, by J. A. McKenzie.

Hull's Opera House, 1893.

Picture Houses

I remember one of the earliest picture houses was located where the Lewis Paint Shop was (west of Eaton's car park). It only operated a few months.

About 1908 the McKenzie brothers (Alex and Archie), built a theatre on the northwest corner of 7th Ave. and Centre St. It was a burlesque house called the Orpheum — no connection with the Orpheum circuit of a later date.

Then there was the Family Theatre on 1st St. W., which is now the Isis (MAC) Theatre. Dr. N. J. Lindsay erected this building. The price of admission for matinees was 5 cents for adults, and children could go in at two for a nickel.

Speaking of theatres, how many knew the history of the cement foundations on 7th Ave. used later by Anderson's parking and car sales lot? About 1913 Col. James Walker owned the property. He had elaborate plans for a large theatre and office building. A start was made, but unfortunately the first war interfered and the building was never completed.

About 1912, Jule and Joy Allan came to town. They first operated the Monarch, then the Rex, just east of the post office, and then built the Allan—now the Strand Theatre.

After Ernie Willis went into the billboard business, W. B. Sherman operated the Lyric. Sir James Lougheed built the Empire Theatre where the Temple-Duff Drug Co. stood.

In The Herald of June 21, 1909, the Empire, which was a vaudeville house, advertised: "John L. Sullivan and Jake Kilrain in person—25c, 35c, 50c." The Pantages vaudeville ran in that theatre for a number of years.

Sir James Lougheed built the Lougheed Building in 1912, which contains the Grand Theatre. The Grand Theatre was operated by W. B. Sherman, and he then called it the Sherman Grand. If my memory is correct, Forbes Robertson opened the theatre, playing in "The Third Floor Back". I remember seeing the great Sarah Bernhardt at the Sherman Grand. In fact most of the famous actors and actresses of that day visited Calgary at one time or another.

As for vaudeville, the Orpheum circuit played Calgary at the Grand for years. I remember about 1908, the famous Madame Melba sang in Calgary. Frank Wrigley, who was organist of Knox Church, underwrote the $6,000 guarantee. Madame Melba sang in the Sherman rink and I remember top price was $5, an unheard-of price for Calgary; but the rink was packed.

The Sherman Rink. How familiar that sounds to all early Calgarians. It was built on 17th Ave. and Centre St. about 1907. A splendid building for a town the size of Calgary in those days. It was operated both as a roller rink and an ice rink. There was, of course, no artificial ice in that day, and all hockey games had to depend upon the weather. All large gatherings were held in the Sherman Rink; political meetings, concerts by noted artists, prize fights and charity balls.

Adjoining the west end there was a large hall used for dancing, amateur plays, etc. At noon, on February 25, 1915, the rink caught fire and burned to the ground.

Did We Have Fun!

After the theatre in our day— boy, did we have fun. When Sir James Lougheed built the Lougheed Building, he certainly looked after the young crowd. We had Cronn's Rathskeller — later called the Plaza — which was located in the basement of the building. It was a long, narrow room, decorated with palms and soft-colored lights, and had a beautiful dance floor. In the background, soft dance music of the highest quality played from 10 oclock till about 2 a.m.

Dance music in those days was very different from today's. I remember one dance orchestra in Calgary featuring a harpist. Imagine a harp playing in a modern orchestra. But back in 1912 it was in keeping with the music of that day.

For about $1.50 you could enjoy a complete evening at the Plaza. They served a three-decker club sandwich, filled with chicken for 50c, with coffee thrown in.

In those days there were no cover charges to contend with. For a couple of dollars a young fellow and his girl could go to the Orpheum Theatre and afterwards dance for an hour or so.

There was one thing about the Plaza that I would like to point out. In those days, there was very little drinking among the young men, and ladies would never think of taking a drink.

The old Plaza had some stirring nights, especially during the first war. Many a young man celebrated his last leave with a party at the Plaza. Personally I was not present, but many have told me of the celebration of Armistice night, Nov. 11, 1918. Some bright youth thought it would be a bright idea to get a live pig, which they did, greased it, and turned it loose on the dance floor. Those present said they did not know which squealed the loudest, the girls or the pig.

Speaking of restaurants: in Calgary about 1909, there was Hoshover's, and did they serve good food! Oysters and steaks were their specialty.

Another wonderful restaurant we had in Calgary was in 1912 when the Hudson's Bay opened their Oak Room on the sixth floor where they served lunches for about 50c. It was a splendid large dining room capable of holding a large number of people. Many banquets were held there in the evenings.

I particularly remember the Burns' anniversary dinners.

Here's a story that my friend Baldy Buck was telling me one time. It seems that out where Baldy Buck ranched years ago, one fall they were forming a school district and one of the school trustees who had been elected by the voters, was formerly a Texas cattleman before ranching in the district. Baldy met the Texan in Calgary at the annual school trustees convention. On the closing day of the convention, Texas Jim said to Baldy, "What are you doing tonight?"

He replied, "Oh, I am going to the Burns' dinner. You had better come along."

"Okay," said Texas Jim, "I am not doing anything."

So they met and away they went to the dinner. At the door they were met by a burly Scot who said to them, "Tickets, gentlemen." Baldy surrendered his ticket but Texas Jim started to walk in. Again the request, "Your ticket please."

Texas Jim looked at the Scot with amazement. "Ticket, ticket, hell! I don't need no ticket to go in here. I've been shipping Pat Burns cattle for years."

CHAPTER 13
Bob Edwards of The Eye Opener

Let me describe a photo I have of an early Board of Trade annual banquet in the Alberta Hotel dining room. Hanging from the ceiling were four large electric fans, long rows of banquet tables were laden with many baskets of fruit and Board of Trade members, many of them hiding behind heavy mustaches and whiskers, were busily gorging themselves on a fifty-cent meal—and what a meal.

When I was a boy, the red letter day of the week was when the family was taken to the Alberta Hotel for Sunday dinner. The old timers in this town all remember the tremendous meals served in the hotels in those days. Hotel managers in those days were big fat fellows.

E. A. Shelley, a well-known Calgarian, started working for the Alberta Hotel as a boy in 1890, and continued until the day it closed.

Ted Shelley has many a story to tell of his experiences. One he tells about the famous Bob Edwards, who often worked all night over at The Herald office on Stephen Ave., just across from the Alberta Hotel. Many a time, about four o'clock in the morning, when Ted would be dozing in the night clerk's chair, he'd be nudged with, "Teddy, me boy, wake up. Teddy, me boy, wake up. I'm dying—get me a drink."

"Go on, Bob," Ted would say, "you know we are closed. I can't get you a drink."

"Teddy, I can't stand it, I tell you, I can't stand it."

So Teddy would get his keys, go into the bar, mix Bob his collins and, shakingly, Bob would drink it. Standing erect, Bob would say, "Ah, Teddy me boy, that's better," and away he would go, to be back in an hour.

One day, years later, Bob Edwards, as was his usual custom, went into Roy Beavers' cafe for dinner. As he finished his dinner, he said to Mr. Beavers, "Roy, there is one cook in this restaurant who really knows his business—I want to congratulate you." Elated, Roy replied, "Well, thank you, Mr. Edwards. Who is that?"

"That is the son of a gun who counted the raisins that went into this pie!"

When we were kids, the Saturday morning that The Eye Openers came out was a big day for us. Bob Edwards himself acted as circulation manager, and stood by, while we youngsters got our papers to sell, joking and teasing with us as well as his customers. And did the papers sell! Often we got a dime or quarter for one Eye Opener.

One of Calgary's early citizens was an architect by the name of J. J. Wilson. Mr. Wilson was known far and wide as "Deafie Wilson" because he was hard of hearing. Deafie Wilson was a constant visitor at the Alberta Hotel. Let anyone say anything to Mr. Wilson, "It's a nice day" or "It's going to rain" — "Don't mind if I do," Deafie would reply and you were stuck for the drinks at the bar.

We, of the present generation living in Calgary, pride ourselves of our western spirit. All Canada admits that there is no town like Calgary.

That spirit did not just happen. The spirit of Calgary is our heritage from the pioneers. That wonderful atmosphere was created in the days of which I speak.

Lords and commoners alike were on an equal footing in Calgary's early history. It did not matter to the old timer which side you came from. It wasn't who you were—but what you were, that counted. And that spirit was fostered for years in the old Alberta Hotel.

Some of His Stories

Bob Edwards was always having fun at the expense of his friends. As an example of his humor, this "society note" appeared in one of his Eye Opener editions (John Mosley, the man concerned, being a popular Calgary hotel man).

"A delightful pink whisky was given Wednesday evening at the hostelry of the Hon. John Mosley, the eminent Conservative leader. The evening was spent in games of progressive black jack, the prizes being boozonnieres and charming cigars. An elegant time was had."

* * * •

One evening a group of fellows were talking about their fishing plans for the opening season.

Here's Bob Edwards' fish story as it appeared in The Calgary Eye Opener, July 2, 1904:

Bob Edwards

Bob Edward's Eye Opener of Oct. 3, 1908.

"The most practical undertaking ever introduced by Englishmen in Victoria was 'beer bottle fishing'. The process is as follows. You fill the boat with as many cases of beer as it will hold and set out to sea. After drinking a bottle you attach a line with a baited hook to the cork, recork the empty bottle and drop it overboard. If blessed with a reasonable thirst you will soon have dozens of bottles bobbing about on the water. When a bottle bobs frantically, you've got a fish.

"By evening your boat is full of fish and you are full of beer.

"This style of fishing is entirely new and no mention is made of it in Isaac Walton's book on the gentle art."

* * *

Another item that Bob Edwards had in his Eye Opener at that time was: "One of the most interesting features of the Calgary Fair is an exhibit of seedless prunes raised in the vicinity of Okotoks."

* * *

In 1906 Calgary had the same problems as we have today — accidents. In The Calgary Eye Opener of March 24, 1906, a little item appears which reads, "Not a life was lost or a buggy smashed at the CPR crossing last week."

Again, under date-line of April 7, 1906, appeared the following: "Calgary's luck is in the ascent. No tragedy occurred this week at the crossing on 1st St. W. This is fools' luck!"

In the Eye Opener of Sept. 8, 1906, this item heads the paper: "Don't get excited, only 14 more weeks of the present city council. Keep cool! Be calm!"

On December 10, 1906:

Dr. Gillespie met a ragged urchin one day in the streets of Glasgow when the following conversation took place.

"Who looks after you, my laddie?"

"Naebuddy."

"Have you no father?"

"Father's deid."

"And your mother?"

"No livin'."

"No sisters?"

"Naw."

"Any brothers?"

"Ay, yin."

"Well, can he no help you; where is he?"

"In Glasgow University."

"How long has he been there?"

"Three years."

"Dear me, three years at the university and can't help his little brother. What is he doing in college?"

"Please, Sir, he's in a bottle. He was born with two heads."

* * *

Innisfail had one major fault, according to Bob Edwards, who was established in Innisfail about the turn of the century when he published The Innisfail Free Lance for a brief time.

Bob Edwards once explained why he left. It seemed the neighbors on his left cut their wood short and the neighbors on his right cut their wood long. Neither size fitted the Edwards' stove. Apparently faced with the horrible prospect of cutting his own wood, Bob Edwards decided to move on.

Another Bob Edwards' story:

An old gentleman, the only undertaker in town, was what might be called a forehanded man. One day he met on the street the young son of a citizen who was reported at death's door.

"How is yer father this morning?" asked the undertaker.

"He's sinking fast," said the son.

"Is that so? Poor boy. By the way, how tall is your father?"

38

CHAPTER 14
Fire Chief "Cappy" Smart

James Smart came to Calgary with his mother, brothers and sister in 1883.

When he first arrived here he worked as a carpenter for about a year or so. Calgary had no undertaker, so James "Cappy" Smart entered that business. His first undertaking parlors were on 8th Ave. between Centre St. and 1st St. E. on the north side of the avenue.

Many are the stories that could be told about James Smart as an undertaker. Situated next door to the undertaking parlors was a barber shop owned by a fellow who did a considerable amount of drinking and who was in the habit of coming into Smart's place, when his own business was slack, and lying down on one of the couches for a sleep.

There was a young boy who went to work for "Cappy" Smart at this time, by the name of Eddy, and the first day that he appeared for work, the barber happened to be having his habitual sleep on the couch. James Smart told Ed-

dy that they had just brought in a corpse and told him to go in and undress him. Eddy got as far as removing the barber's boots when the "corpse" woke up.

In line with every young fellow's ambition in Calgary in those days, "Cappy" Smart joined the fire department and held various positions until he was elected fire chief in 1898, a position he held until his retirement in March, 1933.

During those years he became popularly known as "Cappy", and was active in all civic undertakings. For years he was marshal of the Stampede Parade; and each Christmas Day through those early years, he fired the gun which started The Herald road race. "Cappy" was on every committee that ever entertained any prominent visitor to the city and he always saw to it that the fire department was to the front.

In 1904 the Duke of York (who later became King George V) and his duchess visited Calgary. To welcome them at the station were many Indian chiefs from the vari-

Fire Chief "Cappy" Smart and the first steam engine.

ous reservations. As was their custom when they greeted some dignitary, the chiefs were wearing the official blue coats with brass buttons which had been supplied them by the government.

After being introduced to these chiefs, the duke and duchess approached "Cappy", who stood alongside, attired in his official fireman's navy-blue coat, and were presented to him with these words, "And this, your Highnesses, is Chief Smart."

The duke was heard to remark, "My, what a splendid looking savage." Old timers will tell you that it did not take "Cappy" long to tell his Highness who he was.

Every Boy's Dream

In the early history of this city the activities of the fire department were Calgary's highlights.

It was a social centre, the hub of all sports events, and the firemen promoted every worthwhile community effort that this town had. It was the ambition of every red-blooded young man to belong to the voluntary fire department in those days. By voluntary I mean they worked at other jobs but when the firebell rang, they dropped whatever they were doing and went to the fire.

Firemen were paid 75 cents for each fire they attended and, according to Ed Hall, a well-known Calgary citizen and at one time a voluntary fireman in charge of the roll call, they had 100 per cent attendance for every fire.

Prior to 1885, a bucket brigade existed in the little Western town. The first organization took place in August, 1885, when a hook and ladder company and a bucket corps were organized and a chemical engine obtained.

A few of the names of the first fire department men who became well-known Calgary citizens are: George Constantine who was elected captain for four months (he was followed by Steve Jarrett);

Ed Donahue, was lieutenant; the treasurer was W. H. Cushing; laddermen were Joe Rodway, "Cappy" Smart; hookmen, Jack Summers and Walter Jarrett; axemen, S. N. Jorden and S. J. Clark. The finance committee was formed with Mr. Shaw, J. H. Millward, J. Lambert, John Sullas, Arthur Turnbull and J. Ellis.

In 1885 Calgary had a serious fire which burned out the centre of the town. After this, the department purchased a Ronald engine, 2,000 feet of hose and two hose reels.

In 1886 it was recommended that a fire hall be built.

In 1887, Chief Jarrett resigned and Frank Dick was elected to that position. In May, 1887, the new fire hall was completed and the citizens contributed $500 toward its furnishings. It was finally opened on May 24, 1887, with a concert and dance.

Some of the men whose names appear in the 1887 volunteer fire department list are: James Smart, H. McClellan, A. McTavish, H. Swaffer, A. J. Smyth, John Bremman, R. Fletcher, W. Jarrett, Sol Spafford, James Linton, Thomas Underwood, Archie Grant, and James Jacques.

Volunteer Firefighters

Late in 1887 an incident occurred. The town council became greatly enamored of the new fire hall and proceeded to hold their meetings therein and make it a general place of civic business.

This did not meet with the approval of the voluntary brigade, so Chief Frank Dick and his members stepped down and out, sold their furniture and donated the proceeds to the hospital.

After the brigade resigned, the mayor and council proceeded to appoint a high-salaried chief and, of course, a brigade consisting of the mayor and councilmen and would-be fire fighters.

The new body was well organized on paper but when the time came to control a fire, they weren't in it and in a short time the citizens were clamoring for the reinstatement of the old brigade. On July 23, 1887, at a meeting held in the office of E. R. Rogers, the decision was reached to have the regular brigade take charge again.

On July 29 of the same year, E. R. Rogers was elected chief.

From this time on the brigade forged ahead. In 1890 a set of band instruments was purchased from the Odd Fellows Lodge by D. W. Marsh and presented to the fire department band, together with uniforms and music, etc.

In 1890 new names appeared in the fire department roll: C. F. Comer; my father, J. C. McNeill; L. Earl; J. Wilson and D. Lamond.

In 1892 the names of A. Pearcer, S. L. Saunders, Ralph Bell, and J. S. Roswell were added.

In 1897 a serious flood of the Bow River occurred. The brigade was called out and heroic work was done in rescuing residents from the waterfront.

In 1896 appears the name of H. B. Wilson and on March 7, 1898, "Cappy" Smart was elected head of the brigade.

In 1898, following the May 24 sports event, the brigade undertook to purchase uniforms at a cost of $18 a man. At that time, 30 volunteer firemen belonged to the brigade.

The Firemen's Famous Band

The pride of the Calgary Fire department was its band, under the capable leadership of Crispin E. Smith. Crispin was an Englishman who came to Calgary in the early days and was a splendid musician and band leader, and when conducting, always wore a busby bearskin hat and long Prince Albert coat with white belt and sash.

In 1902 the fire brigade band won the Northwest band competition, at which time it consisted of 35 members—all in uniform. At all special occasions the band would lead the fire brigade in a parade and often formed a guard of honor for visiting dignitaries.

In 1901, through the efforts of Chief "Cappy" Smart and Crispin Smith, the fire department built a bandstand in the CPR gardens—just east of the present site of the Palliser Hotel.

The names of a few of the old brigade should interest many of our citizens today: Bob Bagley,

1889; Everett D. Marshall, 1887; William Ziegler, 1889; Ed Fletcher, 1897; Neil McLaughlin, 1893; Thomas Bruce, 1894; Julian Smart, 1897; Albert Augade, 1897 (Professor Augade, the musician); George Poulton, 1894; Albert Turner, 1897; Michael C. Costello, 1898 (mayor 1915-1918); W. D. Thornton, 1898; Ed C. Hall, 1899; Hiram Worden, 1899; John W. Mitchell, 1900 (mayor 1911-1912); George Henderson, 1900; Daniel J. Lucy, 1900; Fred Tarrant, 1901 (the late Fred Tarrant worked for the Hudson's Bay store's clothing department for years); Lewis H. Murphy, 1901; George M. Gordon, 1901; Alex Creighton, 1902; George S. Gassowski, 1902; **Fred D. McKay**, 1902; Francis Carson, 1902; Ross Lyons, 1902; John McCaffary, 1899; John Smart. 1900; David Cassidy, 1903; Andrew Milne, 1902; Robert MacKay, 1902 (the retired city electric light supt.); Edward Bosswell, 1902; Charles Ferris, 1903; Charlie O' Brien, 1903; Thomas C. Tarrant, 1903; Thomas Smart, 1899.

The glamorous days of the fire department—the days of the galloping fire-horses—the days of the voluntary firemen—the days of the gleaming steam engine (fired by coal) — finally ended in 1911. When the new hall was built on 6th Ave. and 1st St. E., mechanized equipment was introduced and the old horses that we, as children, loved so well—Jimmy and Squibby, Dick and Frank, Bob and Brownie, and the one we thought the grandest of all, old White Wings—were no longer needed; they had served their day and were retired to a well earned rest.

Old White Wings

When they mechanized the fire department, it took away much of the glamor. As a boy, every chance we got we were around the fire hall.

The horses were kept in stalls directly behind the fire reels. When the alarm sounded, automatically the stall doors flew open. The horses were trained to run and stand under their harnesses which were suspended by ropes from the ceiling. Firemen released the harness over the backs of the horses and where so organized that in a record time of 10 seconds a hitching could be made.

At night, the firemen on duty had their clothes so arranged that when they were awakened they could dress and slide down the brass pole in less than a minute

after the alarm rang. Firemen in the early days worked a 24-hour shift with 48 hours off a week.

Harry B. Wilson, a well-known Calgarian, who was secretary of the fire department from 1898-1908, tells of old White Wings, the department's prize horse.

One day Sam Saunders was driving the little chemical wagon with White Wings in the harness. When leaving the firehall, White Wings took too sharp a turn and hit a hole in the road, and Sam was thrown off the cart. White Wings followed the hose wagon ahead to the fire and backed into position—old White Wings did not need a driver.

At the 1908 Dominion Exposition at Calgary, the fire department put on a demonstration in front of the grandstand, to give the public an example of the "horse-sense" of their fire horses.

A team the boys called the "Jack Rabbits" were turned loose on the track. Jack Smart climbed on the hose wagon which had been placed in position with the harness suspended above. Jack hit the gong and immediately the horse ran into position, stuck their necks through the collars, and in seconds the firemen made the hitch and away they went around the track in racetrack time.

Church Burns Down

It was at a downtown fire in 1916—Central Methodist Church was ablaze. Flames were leaping 50 feet in the air — the whole centre of the building was being destroyed. Hundreds were gathered behind the fire-lines; not too close, as the heat was terrific.

A lone figure stood inside the fire lines—a big heavy-faced Scotsman dressed in a dazzling white fireman's coat with a steel helmet to match. In his hand he held a fireman's megaphone; one could hear him bellowing (in gentle language that would curl the hide of an ox) instructions to his men.

Suddenly, near the top of the building, fire belched out of a high window. A fireman high on the tower ladder, directing a stream of water over the top of the cornice, was endangered by the flames.

Instantly the chief instructed the men on another hose line to "let him have it." Tons of water poured on the poor fireman.

Were the sidewalk fire fighters mad! They surged forward yelling at the chief for what he was doing, but they knew better than to come too close, for it would not have been the first time that the chief had directed his firemen to "clear the way."

He had a most effective method of doing this — by turning the water on them. However, the crowd soon realized his action had probably saved the fireman's life, and as the drenched firefighter came down the ladder, a cheer went up.

Who was this white-helmeted, white-coated fire chief? Chief James Smart — "Cappy" to everyone — one of Calgary's most colorful old timers. There was only one "Cappy" Smart! There will never be another!

During "Cappy" Smart's lifetime in Calgary, he was prominent in sports. For years he was referee at all prize fights. I have often heard him at a fight, separating the fighters by telling them to "Break or I'll fight you myself", and he would have been capable.

In the early days the firemen always organized the May 24 sports events.

For March 17, the fire department for years always organized a concert and dance in the Hull Opera House.

There is one thing that can always be said about "Cappy" Smart —he was a fearless firefighter. Three or four times during his life he was seriously injured. He would never send a man where he would not go himself. He was a man who made friends easily and had thousands of friends who had visited this city; once they had met "Cappy" Smart, they never forgot him.

CHAPTER 15
Other Famous Old Timers
I. K. Kerr

The year is 1883. Two men and an Indian guide set out with pack horse on a timber cruise. Let Isaac K. Kerr tell it as recorded in his diary of that date:

"August 16, 1883. Started from Mr. McDougall's at 10 a.m. Crossed Bow River and took the road on south side of river for the mouth of Kananaskis River."

The diary goes on to describe the trip up the Kananaskis through a winding valley between mountains.

"This portion of the valley has a little scattering of Douglas pine, very scrubby, and some groves of small spruce pine. About three miles from our starting point, came through a grove of spruce pine, the largest not to exceed 16 inches on the stump. The last three miles our trail came through a burnt windfall making travelling very slow."

The diary records their trip during August and September of 1883 up the Bow, the Spray and the Kananaskis Rivers. It describes the lakes and rivers; and the estimated stumpage of the various lumber berths. Throughout the diary notations such as these appear:

"The Spray River, said by some to have been so named by the Indians on acount of the spray falls on the Bow at its junction, will make with very little improvement an excellent driving stream."

"Started down trail in search of Spray River. Met A. Patrick who informed us that a stream he took to be the Spray River came in to the Bow opposite Hillsdale Park at about Station 1300."

A. P. Patrick was the early surveyor who died in Calgary at the age of 99 years.

On another page, Isaac describes meeting the agent for Mr. Walker — Col. James A. Walker of Calgary.

On one page of the diary was the following: "At this place we had the pleasure of meeting Sanford Fleming of Ottawa, whom I was informed was once chief engineer of the CPR under the old regime. Also his son, R.S., and George M. Grant, D.D., principal of Queen's University, Kingston, Ont., who were on their way through to the Pacific Coast, but having unfavorable news as to the success of Major Rogers in finding a pass through the Selkirks were somewhat discouraged."

This diary was written in 1883, before the CPR was built through the mountains. Major Rogers was the man after whom Rogers Pass was named.

In another section of the diary their Indian guide, "George Kananaskis," is mentioned. This is doubtless where the Kananaskis River got its name.

Who were these adventurous young lumbermen of 1883? I. K. Kerr and his friend, Dan Donnellan.

In 1883, I. K. Kerr cruised the timber limits that later became the property of the Eau Claire Sawmill Co. Together with Joseph G. Thorpe, Orrin H. Ingram and Alexander McLaren, he leased the timber berths from the Canadian government on April 13, 1884, making an agreement that by the seventh day of July, 1886, they would have erected and in operation a sawmill capable of cutting a thousand feet board measure of lumber each 24 hours for every 2½ square miles of the area licenced.

That was the beginning of the Eau Claire and Bow River Sawmill Co. Peter A. Prince was brought to Calgary from Eau Claire, Wis., as the millwright. Joseph A. Thorpe was the president from 1883 to 1889. I. K. Kerr succeeded him. Mr. Prince was the manager from 1886.

Mr. Kerr was instrumental in founding the Calgary Milling Co. He was president of the Calgary Water Power Co. Ltd.; vice-president of the Canadian Western Gas Co.; a director of Louis Petrie Ltd.; and was active with many other Calgary interests. His home was the former location of the Knights of Columbus clubrooms on 12th Ave. W. He died in Calgary on Tuesday, Dec. 3, 1929, to be remembered as one of the adventurous pioneers whose faith, fortitude and keen business mind helped lay the foundation for Calgary.

J. S. Mackie and P. Turner Bone

During my lifetime in Calgary it has always been a source of surprise to me how many of our early pioneer citizens, coming here 70-80 years ago from the British Isles, retained their native characteristics; many of them never lose their rich brogue, some never lose their soft modulated voices.

They have spent their lives among us, they have done their part to build the West, yet to go into their homes is to go back to the habits and customs of their youth. They have continued year after year to be one of us, yet somehow they have delightfully retained their inborn mannerisms.

One remembers, among many others, my friend of many years, J. S. Mackie. Mr. Mackie was a cultured English-born gentleman of Scottish parentage. Coming to Winnipeg in 1882 and on to Calgary in 1886 — he was mayor of this city in 1901. As mayor he saw the fulfilment of one of his dreams

— the completion of the Calgary-Edmonton railway. He was one of Calgary's successful business men, a furrier, a stationer, later a large real estate operator, the builder of the well-known Lancaster Building in this city.

Mr. Mackie lived his life among us, yet to the day of his death Jan. 21, 1949, he retained that gentle touch, that cultured nature, that we, his friends, so much admired.

Then one remembers P. Turner Bone. Mr. Bone as a young Scottish engineer in 1881, helped survey the CPR. In 1883 he located in Calgary, bought property the very first day the townsite was opened, lived his life among us, yet retained his broad Scottish accent, his Scottish costume. Many have read Mr. P. Turner Bone's memoirs in the book, "When the Steel Went Through," published shortly before his death in 1945.

Old-Time Cattlemen

The following story was told to me by my friend, Bill Wilde of

Red Deer. Mr. Wilde, a native of Banff, in his youth rode the range with some of the bigger cattle outfits and was well versed in cowboy lore.

In the early days the firm of Gordon, Ironside & Fares operated extensively in the West as cattle buyers and shippers. Mr. Ironside lived in Montreal and looked after the export business. J. T. Gordon lived in Winnipeg and William Fares was the cattle buyer in charge of western operations.

It was customary once a year for the three men to meet in Winnipeg to discuss the year's business. At one of these meetings the firm's credit manager said to Mr. Fares, "Bill, you gave a cheque last year to a man (we'll call him Smith) at Bassano for some cattle you bought and the cheque hasn't been cashed. Will you find out about it?" Mr. Fares, on his next trip didn't happen to see Smith the rancher, and once again that fall, the credit man spoke of the cheque which hadn't been cashed.

The second year, Mr. Fares went to see Smith, and on approaching him on the matter, he found the rancher reluctant to talk. Finally the old rancher told him and in a confidential manner asked Mr. Fares not to mention it to anyone. "I lost the damn thing somewhere," said Smith. "Must have burned it in an old pair of overalls."

"Yes," replied Mr. Fares, "but that's all right. I'll issue you another cheque."

"No, be damned," said the rancher, "you paid for them cattle once, and you ain't a-goin' to pay for them again."

Charlie Jackson and the Cashmans

Charlie Jackson, who came here in 1882 and homesteaded in what is now the Killarney district, was Calgary's first milkman. The milk supply came from two wild cows from the cattle of Sam Livingston. Years later old timers kidded Charlie about the picture of his first milk wagon, a little two-wheel cart. The picture was taken in front of the town pump!

Charles C. Jackson was a wonderful old timer. He was one of the founders of the Salvation Army Corps here and did much to promote that institution's interests. I well remember with my father, visiting Charlie in the hospital about 1911. Charlie had broken two ribs in the most unusual way.

At that time Charlie was interested in the garage business. They had just received a new open model touring car. Charlie was sitting in the back seat; the driver went over a bad bump in the road; Charlie went up in the air, the car went from under him and Charlie landed on the hard ground.

To my mind, Calgary's prize business advertiser was a clothing man by the name of Dan Cashman. His favorite ad was the picture of the back of his head on which was written, "Meet me face to face in Dan Cashman's store". And another, "If you don't know Dan Cashman, you ought to". Once he advertised a sale of men's trousers with the following caption, "Men's pants are down again."

His brother, Frank Cashman, was possibly one of the kindest men who ever came to this city. He arrived here in 1908 and was in business with Dan until 1912.

During the cold winter months it was Frank's custom to have a

Charlie Jackson in what was said to be Calgary's first car.

late supper in the Club Cafe. Afterwards he would walk down 8th Ave. to 2nd St. E. and back up 9th to the depot. When he met a fellow who looked down on his luck Frank would ask him, "Are you broke?" "Have you a place to sleep?"

If the chap needed help, Frank would proceed to write out an order on a hotel for a bed, using the firm's business card, and often as not a slip for a meal.

My friend, Frank McHugh, who told me the story says that he had been with Frank Cashman when Frank gave out 10 or 12 orders. McHugh asked him one time, "Frank, doesn't it cost you a lot?"

"Yes," replied Frank, "but it's a great satisfaction to have a few of them later come into the store, repay me, and buy a few clothes."

Speaking of charity, did you ever hear of the "Samis Woodpile"? When A. J. Samis was the city commissioner, early in this century,

the town had a woodpile on 8th Ave. East. When men out of work in those days wanted a meal or bed, they earned it by an hour's work cutting wood.

To us youngsters, the most famous woodpile in Calgary was in the back yard of R. J. Hutchings' home. Mr. Hutchings had his own creed about bringing up his boys and the boys in the neighborhood.

In our day, when we needed a dime or a quarter, one way to earn it was to crosscut saw stove lengths in the Hutchings' back yard — one cent for each saw cut. When we had cut our allotment, down we would troop to Mr. Hutchings' private office in the Great West Saddlery, and solemnly he would pay us, always taking our word for the count.

Sons or sons' friends were always treated alike. Harold Carson, Norman Mackie, Malcolm McAra, Jack, Doug, Harry, George and Stewart Hutchings were a few of the gang. A wonderful man, Mr. Hutchings, don't you think?

R. C. Thomas

Friday, June 9, 1950, will be long remembered by me, for that day I lost a friend, a friend of many years. But before I tell you his name, let us go back 66 years.

In 1883 a young Welshman arrived in Calgary, at that time western end of the CPR. For a $10 bill my friend took up a homestead of 160 acres, down the Bow River 17 miles. By hand he dug and put in his small crop, built himself a shack and began his great adventure. During the Riel Rebellion in 1885 he teamed and made a stake of $1,200. Moving to Calgary, he located on the corner of 8th Avenue and 2nd Street West, buying the corner for $1,500 ($500 cash) and opened a livery business. From there he branched into a coal and wood yard. A powerful man, my friend, delivering his own coal by the ton. Years later he often told me how a lady asked him in for a cup of tea, how that woman high-hatted him. Believe me, he knew their names and never forgot, nor forgave. From livery, coal and wood he went into to ice business. The original ice houses were located on 7th Avenue between 2nd and 3rd Streets West. By now my friend had many interests — coal, lumber, livery stables, ice, and with it, property. His business interests grew with the development of the city until he became one of Calgary's leading capitalists. But with all his wealth, he remained a man of simple tastes, a modest man, a devoted friend. My heart is heavy, for on June 9, 1950, I helped carry my friend, R. C. Thomas, to his last resting place.

Roy Beavers' Snakes

This is the tale of snakes; big boa constrictors, little coral snakes and slimy cobras, all trained so they would crawl around a circus man's neck. It was one of the attractions of the 1908 Dominion Fair at Calgary.

The snake tent was located just where the Victoria Park Administration building stands today. Out in front of the snake pit stood a little hot-dog stand—a comparatively new invention at that time. Cooking the hot-dogs was a young fellow we will call Roy.

While the hot-dogs were frying, Roy would, in his husky, comical manner, alternately bark: "Come one, come all, see the greatest snake show on earth — Here pardner, have a hot-dog while you watch that wonderman, Recker, and his trained live snakes." Roy and his partner, Recker, had quite a week.

In a few days Roy had absorbed the free and easy way of Calgary, and made up his mind that it was here he would stay, and stay he did, although Recker and his snakes went on to farther fields. Roy hustled about and got a store on 8th Ave. just east of the present Maclean Block. He made enough money to set himself up in a small restaurant business and through the years grow with the town.

Roy was a great one to advertise. One stunt he pulled in 1911 was to put on a dinner one Sunday where nothing was served but wild game: duck, goose, antelope or buffalo. (Roy says he had to cook the buffalo meat for days.) To attract customers, Roy hung the carcasses of two large antelope outside, one on either side of the door.

But Roy had fun. He has had fun all his life in Calgary and what is more, he made it pay!

Most of you have probably guessed by now who I am talking about. For those who have not, he was that popular Calgary booster—Roy Beavers.

Early Drummers

Following the arrival of the CPR, a group of men invaded this West.

In the '90s and the early part of this century, life in the West was one of adventure and at times presented real hardships.

These early drummers (salesmen) were a friendly lot who soon knew everybody and were known by everyone. The railway men were their friends and thought nothing of allowing these fellows to flag their trains; often they would wait for 10 minutes or so, while one of these men ran around town. The livery men, Johnny Hamilton, Ike Ruttle, and others, drove them about in open democrats during the summer and in open sleighs piled high with buffalo robes in the winter.

As a group, they were a happy lot. They laughed at misfortune and grinned at their luck. They played tricks on newcomers to their fraternity, but always lent a helping hand in the event of real difficulties.

A few were heavy drinkers, but the majority were teetotalers; nine out of ten smoked cigars.

They thought nothing of being tied up for days in some village. They knew no working hours and often worked until midnight.

The tricks they played on each other are legends.

One evening when in Lethbridge, one of their members succumbed to the effects of "a gay evening", so the boys laid him out on a couch, covered his face with talcum, lugged up the palm trees that decorated the rotunda and left the poor guy holding a lily.

Who were these fellows? That grand group of men, the commercial travellers.

Their names tell the story of the commercial life of Calgary. Their hard work made Calgary the finest distributing point in Western Canada. Many became our first citizens, establishing businesses that became the backbone of this city.

Just to mention a few: William (Bill) Georgeson, John Horne, Archie McKillop (one of the first to bring racehorses to Calgary), E. A. Dagg, Sam Savage, Tug Wilson, A. B. Sproat, Howard Heisler, R. J. Hutchings (one of the members of the first incorporated city council), W. H. Berkinshaw, Alf. Russell, Bill Dunlop, Bill Crossley, A. W. McGuire, Mart Taylor, Harry Madill, Bob Watson, Tom Martin, Joe McMullen, George Christie, Tom Dawson, Ernie Thom, Harry Reynolds, Bill Logan, Scotty Adams, Arley Folkins, Dick Marriott, George Kelloway, Archie Monatt, and J. W. Speer, who drove the first car used by a traveller in Calgary.

These men and many others (for I have only mentioned a few from memory) pioneered the West the hard way.

A travellers' association which was started years ago, met for one day each year in Calgary during the Christmas season; they were known as "The Fourteen Old-Time Salesmen". All of these fourteen have made their last trip, but their successors enthusiastically carry on.

Pioneers and Old Timers Association

Many Calgarians must wonder how the Southern Alberta Pioneers' and Old Timers' Association came into being.

We have to thank the Calgary Rotary Club for the founding of our association. On Dec. 28, 1920, the Calgary Rotary Club, under the presidency of W. R. Marshall, issued invitations to their members to invite to a luncheon friends who had, at that time, been residents of the province for 30 years or more. The outcome was one of the most momentous luncheons that the Calgary Rotary Club had ever held — some 190 guests being present.

As a result of this luncheon, which lasted until nearly 6 p.m., the old timers decided to form an association.

The minutes of the Calgary Rotary Club record the following:

"The ball room of the Palliser was filled to capacity when the meeting started. Introductions of the guests were made and many amusing incidents were recorded. Cliff Andrews, a member of the Rotary Club, disguised with a long beard and dressed in a frock coat, was introduced as the mythical character created by Bob Edwards of The Calgary Eye Opener, Peter J. McGonigal, and completely fooled most of those present.

CHAPTER 16
The First School Teacher

J. W. Costello, father of the well-known Costello family of Calgary, was Calgary's first school teacher. The first school class was held in the Boynton Hall which was located approximately where the present Variety Theatre stands.

The first building erected for school purposes was a little one-room school on the corner of 9th Ave. and 5th St. E. The building is now on St. George's Island.

The next school was a small building located on 8th Ave. E., where the Safeway Store stands today, and classes were taught by James Spencer Douglas.

The first permanent building

erected for school purposes was Central School which stood on the present location of James Short School. The original building was a four-room brick veneer school. Joseph Boag was first principal, and was succeeded later by that well-known citizen, James Short, K.C.

By 1885, the separate school system was inaugurated in the Roman Catholic mission.

Early Calgary students had plenty of outside activity. In the winter they skated on Frank Claxton's ice rink — a covered rink no less — that was situated on 6th Ave. and Centre St.

Incidentally, in the evenings

Calgary citizens skated to music played by the Mounted Police band. Claxton's rink was later torn down when the Hull Opera House was built.

In the summer of 1885, the chief sport was to watch the cowboys breaking horses at Sandy Mac-Donald's stable situated on 8th Ave. where the Strand Theatre is today.

After 1900, when I personally attended Central School, our chief afternoon sport was to swim in an indoor swimming pool, the Calgary Swimming Bath, located on 5th Ave. across from the school.

I remember the winter of 1905-06 when the little Baptist Church, which was located where the Greyhound Building stands today, burned down.

It was zero weather and, while the firemen were fighting the fire, ice formed on the churchsteps. For the balance of the winter, every youngster in town used those steps for a slide which carried them right across 7th Ave. to an open field where the present Hudson's Bay Co. stands.

Indian School

While in Ed Hall's hardware store one day, I was talking with an Indian sub-chief, Ben Calf Robe, of the Blackfoot tribe. He was telling me of the white man who taught him our way of life, Rev. G. H. Hogbin, principal of the Calgary Industrial Indian School. How many citizens know that we had an Indian school in this city in the '90s? It was located near the Bow River, close to the

Rev. John McDougall (sitting, left), Chief Samson, James Seenum, Rev. R. B. Steinhauer, and Jonas Goodstoney, 1886.

present site of the nitrogen plant.

At that time there were more than 100 Indian boys in residence each year: young Indians from various tribes — the Sarcees, the Bloods of Cardston, the Peigans of Brocket, the Blackfoot of Gleichen and Cluny.

What struck me most forcibly was the respect which Ben Calf Robe held for Mr. Hogbin and the credit he gave him. How many of us remember the name of our teacher of 50 years ago?

I was asking Ben Calf Robe about the teepees which are set up on the Exhibition grounds each year during Stampede Week — what the paintings on the canvas represent, and was given the following information:

Each teepee belongs to a family and they are very proud of the sketches and drawings on their homes. Indian families honor their ancestors and on each teepee you will notice the heraldry of the Indian in their "coat-of-arms" painted on the panels of these lodgings.

For example: the Three Suns family use the symbol of "Three Suns"; the Bear Robe family use the design of a buffalo with an Indian arrow piercing the animal.

The paintings on the panels represent the history of the family life. They may have been a family of warriors or hunters, and it is all written there in Indian sign language — their daring, pluck and skill are all recorded.

Indians believe in spiritual powers of animals.

The medicine men of the tribes are the "song leaders" — they know the songs and ceremonies of their individual tribes, and are the leaders at sun dances — now very different from the original sun dances.

The Venerable Archdeacon J. W. Tims was the man who was credited with being the influencing force that finally persuaded the Blackfoot tribe to give up the cruel sun dance that was practised before 1883 — a gruelling spectacle where young braves tore rawhide thongs through the flesh of their breasts.

Indians are a proud race and have an ancient and historic background.

Indian council meetings are a serious affair. The Indians adhere to their ritual which is as rigid as any Christian order, and their altar in the centre is respected with the greatest of dignity.

CHAPTER 17
"Mother" Fulham

Many of my friends have said to me, "I thought you were going to tell us about Mrs. Fulham."

Well, I guess I stuck my neck out by mentioning her name, so here goes! This is against my better judgment, for Mrs. Fulham's ghost is liable to haunt me. I remember vividly how frightening the mere mention of her name was

to us as children. Our mothers had a very effective way of "boxing our ears" — "If you kids don't behave, I'll tell Mrs. Fulham to come and get you." What a character she was.

Mrs. John Fulham (and sometimes her husband, but not often) lived in a little house in Section 16, just west of the Court House, on Angus Avenue (now 6th Ave. W.). At the rear of the property in an old stable she kept a cow and some pigs. The pigs tell the story.

To feed them she gathered the swill daily from the hotel kitchens downtown—the Royal, the Grand Central, the Alberta, the Palace, the Windsor, the Queen's, the Criterion Cafe, the New Brunswick Cafe and others. To gather the swill, she attached a large swill barrel to the back of a little democrat she drove. Her pony she called Billy.

Mrs. Fulham was of Irish descent, quick-tempered, quick-witted and strong. Old timers have seen her lift, single-handed, a heavy barrel of refuse into her wagon— it wouldn't matter if a little slopped over. In fact she was a holy terror driving down Stephen or Atlantic Avenue roaring in her Irish brogue, the women and children all afraid of her, the men just a little bit nervous, for they never knew who she would turn on next.

Chief English and his two policemen—Jim Frazer and Bob Barker (the entire police dept.) often had some interesting experiences with her.

Crispin Smith, the magistrate, would fine her, warn her, threaten her, but it didn't do any good. She likely realized that "Calgary's Justice Department" was just having a lot of fun—as it was. When things really got tough she had P. J. Nolan defend her. The famous Paddy Nolan, himself an Irishman, had fun too.

For instance, there was the time the CPR train killed her cow. The story goes that she sued the CPR. The lawyers were arguing about the legality of a "No Trespassing" sign that they claimed was prominently displayed on the CPR right-of-way. Mrs. Fulham listened as long as she was able to hold her tongue and then asked them, "Do you damn fools think me cow could read?"

Even the CPR officials were wary of Mrs. Fulham, and well they might be, for, as the story goes, she actually went into the private car of the president of the CPR and accused him of killing her cow. It is reported that the president told her they would get her another cow. Not being satisfied with that, Mrs. Fulham asked him where he was going to get a cow as good as her Nellie—she gave six quarts of milk a day.

Bill Niven, a local CPR engineer, told of the time J. N. Niblock, the CPR superintendent, had him up on the carpet. "Billy," said the superintendent, "were you one of the boys that put the shafts of Mrs. Fulham's democrat through the CPR fence and hitched her pony on the other side." Bill replied innocently, "No, Mr. Niblock, it wasn't me."

There was a CPR conductor by the name of Bill Birchell, who used to carry itching powder, and once in a while when Stephen Avenue was quiet, unknown to Mrs. Fulham, he would rub a little powder on her pony. Swill, democrat, Irish temper and Mrs. Fulham's picturesque language would cause a young riot.

Then there are the stories all old timers tell. The time Mrs. Fulham hurt her leg and went to Dr. H. G. Mackid for treatment. "I'll bet you $5, Mrs. Fulham, that there isn't a dirtier leg than that in Calgary," the doctor said. "And be sure, I'll take you," replied Mrs. Fulham, and proceeded to show Dr. Mackid her other leg. Dr. Mackid paid.

And the time she caught a Chinaman looking in her swill barrel at the rear of the Alberta Hotel. She dumped the poor

Chinaman into the barrel head-first.

Mrs. Fulham had some property around town and Tony Grogan was her financial agent. He tells of the time she went into The Herald printing office and upset a couple of cases of hand type because she was told that Mr. Braden hadn't put an ad in the paper as he had promised her.

Mrs. Fulham herself could neither read nor write.

Mrs. William Niven, wife of the CPR engineer, tells me that the first time she saw Mrs. Fulham was in 1889—the day was July 12. As was their custom in those days, the Orange Lodge had a parade, but the attraction on that day in 1889 was not the Orangemen.

Although Mrs. Fulham did not belong to the Orange order, she was dressed up for the occasion, but not in orange color! She had gone into the Hudson's Bay Company store and obtained a wide silk paddy-green ribbon and draped it from her neck to her knees, topped with a huge green bow. As the parade passed she staged a one-woman show, shouting her caustic remarks, telling those Orangemen what she thought of them.

"Cappy" Smart always claimed that after Mrs. Fulham left Calgary, she settled in Vancouver, where she ran a little restaurant on the waterfront. He claims to have eaten a meal at her place. No old timer ever believed "Cappy's" story—but maybe he was not kidding!

My friend, Baldy Buck, tells me of the time the boys took Mrs. Fulham to the annual Fireman's Ball, the social event of the season, according to Baldy. Mrs. Fulham wore a long evening ensemble of brilliant paddy-green. The fun for Baldy that memorable evening was the hour the boys spent with Mrs. Fulham in the balcony overlooking the dancers. Baldy says Mrs. Fulham knew a choice bit of gossip about everyone present and presented it in her own picturesque language.

CHAPTER 18
First Train Crews

Calgary, in the early days before 1900, did not mean very much as a railway town. Gleichen and Canmore were the divisional points and train crews lived in those towns. Calgary was only a coaling station. Through-trains coaled-up at the location where the Palliser Hotel stands today, using a windlass and hand buckets.

In 1896 there was one railway crew living in Calgary: Joe Barnes, the engineer; and Jimmy Faulkner, the fireman.

Early in 1897, Calgary boasted two crews: Joe and Jimmy; and Archie McLeod and William Niven.

The C. & E. branch to Edmonton ran three mixed trains a week which left Calgary at 8 a.m. and arrived at Edmonton at 5 p.m. and on the Macleod branch there were also three trains a week.

Calgary's first CP station, 1884. Left to right: R. G. Marsh, station agent; W. T. Ramsay, land agent; T. B. Braden, Calgary Herald founder; G. E. Jacques, first watchmaker; and CP Constable Foy.

D. J. Young, a well-known Calgarian, told me of his experiences as a passenger on those early trains to Edmonton. On one summer trip the weeds were so high along the right-of-way (there were no graveled roadbeds as today) that the train crew had to stop to cut the weeds because the wheels of the train were "greasing" the track when running over these weeds and the engine driving wheels just spun around.

I asked him what the passengers were doing. "Oh, just out picking flowers, throwing rocks, browsing around."

In 1897, Calgary boasted three train crews: Paule Elcombe, an engineer, and George Monilaws, a fireman, as well as the other two crews.

In 1898, the year the Klondyke gold rush started, the C. & E. train did quite a business. Hundreds went overland via Edmonton with their equipment and dog-teams, but

many never reached Dawson. It was that year the CPR started a daily service to Edmonton.

When the south route was first built, the CPR only went as far as Macleod. From there to Lethbridge the stage coach was the only means of public transportation. Before the CPR built the high-level bridge at Lethbridge in 1907, the railroad ran from Macleod to St. Mary's and back to Lethbridge.

Mrs. William Niven vividly remembers the flood of 1902. She left Macleod to come to Calgary.

How long do you think it took her? Twenty-one days! The main line of the CPR was washed out. The engineer and fireman took a hand car and went from Nanton, where the train was stalled, to High River to get supplies. The boys were able to obtain just one case of beer and two dozen eggs in a paper bag.

When they reached the stranded

A CP passenger train at Calgary depot, 1889.

train crew and passengers, most of the beer had disappeared and the boys were in a happy mood. Holding up the bag of eggs, the engineer said, "Look folks, fresh eggs."

The paper bag by that time was much the worst for wear and the precious eggs dropped to the ground. Incidentally, one of those passengers was a little boy of nine or 10 years of age, Harold (Torchy) Anderson, who was formerly a reporter for The Calgary Herald and later the editor of The Vancouver Province.

CHAPTER 19
The Calgary Herald, 1883

While going into The Herald Building, the thought struck me: "Why, you're overlooking one of the best old-time tales right here!"

What of the background of this newspaper, The Herald?

Like the city of Calgary, The Herald started from scratch. You have all read, or will read, how The Herald came to Calgary; when A. M. Armour and T. B. Braden printed the first weekly paper in 1883, using a little Washington hand press; when The Herald office was located in a tent on the banks of the Bow River; how they started with one newsboy. Today they have 1200 newsboys.

It would be easy for me to go to The Herald library, set up the microfilm and copy from the files of The Herald; but, on thinking it over, I remember that there are two well known Calgarians who worked as journeyman printers with The Herald in 1890, Harry B. Wilson (died 1954) and John D. McAra (died 1966) who went into business for himself.

John McAra came to The Herald in 1890, having served his apprenticeship under the famous

Nicholas Flood Davin of The Regina Leader-Post, who started his paper in 1883.

McAra tells me that in 1890 The Herald was owned by a group of Calgary men, George Alexander, G. C. King, and others, who purchased it from Alex Lucas, Sir James Lougheed and M. S. McCarthy, who had previously bought the newspaper business from Hugh Cayley in 1886.

In 1890, the manager and editor was J. A. Reid. Frank Livingston was news editor; George Grogan (a brother to Tony) was office manager; the journeyman printers were Heck Ross, H. B. Wilson, Everett Marshall, Martin Hodgkins ("The Duke"), and John D. McAra. That year, The Herald was published in a small building just east of the old Club Cafe. To one side was the firm of Fitz-gerald and Lucas, and to the other was a restaurant called the Bodego.

In those days the printers were paid by "piece work" and they earned from $16 to $18 a week and worked a 54-hour week.

In 1892 the boys went on strike; not for more wages but because the manager, J. A. Reid had failed to pay them at all. The strike was soon settled when the directors discovered what was the trouble, and they arranged for weekly pay envelopes.

Times were tough and often the boys were asked to accept script orders on the paper's advertisers. John McAra told me he had a very convenient arrangement. He boarded with Mrs. D. W. Moore on Reinach Avenue; she bought her groceries from the Hudson's

The Calgary Herald was started in a tent on Aug. 31, 1883. Left to right: unidentified, Andrew M. Armour (founder); NWMP Constable Tom Clarke; T. B. Braden (co-founder).

Bay Co., who in turn advertised in The Herald.

All type was hand set and the press was hand fed. John McAra well remembers the day the first power-press was installed. It was a steam operated, cumbersome arrangement; the boiler alongside. One of the duties of the printers was to stoke up the boiler with wood; this was fine in the winter, but plenty hot in the summer.

News from the East was received over a press wire, but it had its disadvantages, for when the paper neglected payments, because they lacked funds, they often found a dead wire. When that happened, the editorial staff relied on Eastern newspapers for their material.

Charlie Smith's Yarns

The other day a friend said to me, "I thought you were going to tell some stories in these articles you are writing for The Herald."

Well, here's one for my friend.

Charles O. Smith, at the time of this story, in 1925-26, was editor of The Calgary Herald. He was one of Calgary's most popular business men and always had a host of stories. As an after-dinner speaker he was very much in demand.

In 1926 the old timers were honored to have him on their program at the annual banquet at the Palliser Hotel. In his response to the toast to the press, here is the story he told.

In Edmonton, after 1890 and before the High Level Bridge was built, the only CPR station was in Strathcona, now South Edmonton. Passengers for Edmonton got off on the south side and were driven to Edmonton via the Low Level Bridge. At that time there was an old time character by the name of Buckskin Bill who drove a buckboard across the coulee.

The Hon. Frank Oliver was an early newspaperman in Edmonton, coming there in 1878 as publisher of The Edmonton Bulletin. One day in the early '90s an eminent Englishman, just out from the Old Country, got off the CPR train at Strathcona and was being driven by old Bill across to Edmonton.

Bill sat there smoking his pipe, the shaggy cayuses jogging along.

The Englishman spoke, "I say, I say, my man, your team is very anaemic."

Bill, a little deaf, cocked his ear and asked, "What's that?"

The Englishman repeated, "I say, I say, your team is very anaemic —very bloodless."

"Well, that's damn funny," said Bill, "only yesterday, I took Frank Oliver across and he told me I had the bloodiest team he's ever seen."

Charlie Smith enlivened any gathering he attended. He was a regular contributor to the fun at the weekly Rotary Club luncheons. One Christmas he made a presentation to the wife of the president. Charlie had gone over to the tent factory and had them make a pair of ladies' bloomers out of stiff striped canvas. When the good lady opened the large, fancy, decorated Christmas box, she took out her gift. The bloomers stood up by themselves. He was always playing tricks on his friends.

When my friend reads this he will feel like the Indian woman who had been drinking and the old timer said to her, "Squaw, you have been taking too much liquor."

She replied, "No, a little too much is just enough."

CHAPTER 20
Electric Lights in 1893

Surprising as it may seem, by 1891 Calgary had two electric light companies supplying electricity to the town: the Calgary Electric Company, situated on McIntyre Ave., and the Calgary Water Power Company, situated on the Bow River, a subsidiary of the Eau Claire Lumber Co.

The two companies supplied approximately 2,500 lights.

The rivalry between the two companies gave Calgary the cheapest light in Canada at that time. It would not be very cheap according to standards today, however. The cost was from 40 to 50 cents a month for a single 16-candle-power lamp.

It is also surprising to know that as early as 1890 Calgary had a water system. George Alexander was the president of the Calgary Waterworks Company. Several miles of pipe had been laid by this time, and a pumping station was located on the banks of the Bow River on the east side of Louise Bridge.

There was one thing in Calgary in the early days that all had to contend with, and that was mud. In my youth, Stephen Ave. was plank sidewalked and the mud on the street in the springtime was terrific. I remember well that they used to scrape it up with horse-drawn scrapers into great piles in the centre of the street.

In the block by the City Hall, along 7th Ave., there was a slough. Well I remember this slough, for as a boy I lived on the corner of 6th Ave. and 3rd St. W. My father and Walter Claxton were partners in owning a cow. Walter kept and milked the cow morning and evening at his place on 7th Ave., just east of the present Colonial Hotel. It was my job to go after the milk each evening, and believe me, it was a long way in those days from 1st St. E. to 3rd St. W., especially in the winter time — and worse still in the spring mud.

I remember the wooden sidewalks on Reinach and Northcote Aves. were wired together, otherwise they would have floated away in the spring floods. In Calgary's early history the Bow River overflowed its banks every spring. Low lying areas from about the present Centre St. to 6th St. E. up to 5th Ave. were always in danger.

About 1900 the river was diked, and this helped materially in times of high water.

CHAPTER 21
History of Motor Cars

This is the story of motor cars in Calgary from 1909 to 1914. The names of those early cars read like a fairy tale when compared with today's standard names.

Do you remember the Rambler, Rocket-Schneider, Russell, Russel-Knight, Haynes, Locomobile, Simplex, American Underslung, White, White Steamer, Kissel, Kitton, Maxwell, Overland, MacLaughlin-Buick, Pearce-Arrow, Peerless, Mercer, Pope-Toledo, Benz, Christie, Cino, Premier (electric gear shift), Stearns, Wilcox, the E.M.F., King 8, Cord, Lexington Six, Saxon, Chalmers, Norwalk, McFarlane, Mitchell, Lancaster, Wolseley, Sunbeam, Winton, Hotcris, Stutz, Stoddart-Dayton, Apperson, Franklin?

Calgary had them all in her prosperity from 1909 to 1916.

The first so-called garage started operation about 1906 in a converted barn situated on 7th Ave. just west of Centre St. Next door to this was a tire shop operated by George Gillespie who was Calgary's first tire man. Later he moved his shop to 6th Ave. where the Gas Company is located today.

In 1909, F. L. Irving, with his brother, Ernie, and George Hanna, opened the Central Garage on 6th Ave. and 2nd St. E. That same year Roy Lee opened the Maxwell agency (the Diamond Motors) on 6th Ave. W. where the Modern Motors were later located.

In 1910 Julien Chatel built the Mount Royal Garage on 17th Ave. and 5th St. W. where he sold the Rocket-Schneider car. Alderman L. White built the White Motors on 9th St. and 16th Ave. W. MacLeod and Williamson built the Cadillac Garage on 15th Ave. which is now the location of the Detroit Auto Body Works. 1910 was also the year the MacLaughlin-Buick people built their showrooms and garage on the corner of 7th Ave. and 3rd St. W.

In 1911 a French car manufacturing company sent a young mechanic out from France. He became a Calgary citizen and was active in the garage business, A. A. Julien.

Jack Austin of General Supplies ran a garage for the Motor Livery on 3rd St. W. between 4th and 5th Avenues.

O. S. Chapin built the Overland Garage on 5th Ave. W., and showrooms on 8th Ave. W. He also had the agency for Packards.

The Mitchell Garage was located on 11th Ave.

The Ford Motors built next door. There was a young fellow called Ernie (E. A. McCullough), who had the idea he could sell Ford cars. He became president of Maclin Motors, and an alderman.

The Russell Garage was on 15th Ave. E. at the present location of the Red Cross headquarters. Carl Grasswick was on 6th Ave. E.

I. K. Kerr built the Kerr Motors on 17th Ave. W. across from the Western Canada High School. His son, H. H. Kerr, had the agency for the Kissel and Kitton cars.

About 1912, Norman Lougheed built the Western Motors cn 11th Ave. W. where the Canadian Fairbanks-Morse Co. was located.

The Studebaker Garage was built of Calgary sandstone on 16th Ave. and 8th St. W. in 1913 by Charlie Jackson.

The McIntosh Garage was located on 5th Ave. between Centre and 1st St. W. They were the agents for English cars.

The first car in this district was a little steam car owned by the Cochrane Ranch. Charlie Jackson bought it from them and it is this car he drove in the Calgary Stampede parade for many years.

To my knowledge, the first car in Calgary was owned by J. E. Prince of the Eau Claire Lumber Co. Well I remember being driven uptown by Johnny Prince in 1905.

Dr. J. S. McEachern had an early model Buick then, as well as Archie McKenzie, whose car had the door at the centre rear.

About 1907, Calgarians started buying cars in earnest, and by 1914 there were all models. Calgary was prosperous: most of the larger cars in those days cost $5,000 to $6,000; tires and repairs were also expensive. Julien Chatel brought in 12 Rocket-Schneider cars and sold them all for $5,000 to $6,000 apiece.

John Sharples was a man who traveled a great deal in cars, and for five consecutive years Mr. Sharples spent from four to six months touring Europe with his chauffeur George who told me that for a period of more than ten years, when they were not in Europe, Mr. Sharples and he toured the United States and Eastern Canada.

Freddy Lowes was a great one for cars. In 1912 he owned an American Underslung and two Pearce-Arrows, which cost $5,000 apiece. While in California for the winter of 1912-13, he attended an auto race in Santa Monica. The car that won the race was built by the Mercer Co., and Freddy bought it — price was no object. He brought it to Calgary, but was not able to have much fun with it here as there were no roads for a racing car in those days.

I remember the big Pearce-Arrow, robin-egg-blue roadster owned by J. A. Robertson, the real estate man.

Mr. Robinson of the Motor Livery owned a Locomobile. Cars are not made that big today.

Norman Lougheed had a chain-driven Pope-Toledo — it was a lot of automobile.

I could go on naming cars and their owners, but I want to tell you of the experiences of a well-known cattleman who was in the car business also. In 1911 he financed three Peerless cars for a garageman, each costing about $5,000. Two of them were sold, but the third one was stored for 38 years and in 1949 was sold as a museum curiosity for $750. The cattleman wisely stayed with the cattle business and did not worry much about his experiences in the car market. His name was Frank Collicutt.

In 1912-13 we had the famous Barney Oldfield in Calgary. In 1912, he raced at Victoria Park, along with two other drivers. The cars they used were the Blitzen-Benz, Cino and Christie.

A. A. Jullien tells me that their average speed was about 55 miles an hour. In 1913, Barney Oldfield returned to Calgary and raced at Trotter's farm near Shepard, where he averaged a mile in 23 seconds on a straight-away track, driving a Christie car.

Amateur races were held at Victoria Park in 1912. A. A. Jullien drove a Rocket-Schneider; Carl Grasswick an American Underslung; a fellow named Domary a Stearns; and Jim O'Brien a Stoddart-Dayton. Jullien won the race.

In 1913 an amateur race was held at Trotter's farm with the same drivers. Mr. Jullien says the entrance fee was $100 — winner take all. Jullien won again. He told me he bought a new hat that night.

Another amateur race was held at Victoria Park that year. Jullien won two of these races and Carl Grasswick won the third.

In 1913, Bob Burman, another famous driver, demonstrated at Victoria Park with a Blitzen-Benz.

In 1917 a popular Calgarian, Fred Seigel, was killed in an auto race at Victoria Park.

How many old timers remember the big McFarlane roadsters driven by George Brick, the oil man?

CHAPTER 22
The Bull Teams

In preceding articles, I have talked about automobiles in 1910. It's fantastic but true that just 30 years previous to that date, the vast majority of freighting and transportaion into the North West Territories was done by oxen, or "bull teams" as they were commonly called. The old trails are still visible in many parts of southern Alberta.

In the '70s and early '80s, aside from the stage coaches that carried the mail and few passengers, the covered wagon that brought in some settlers, the country depended on oxen.

The bull teams — where did they come from, how were they trained, who drove them, and how? Some of the most interesting characters in this country in the early days were men associated with "bull team" freighting.

Many old timers knew D. W. Davis, the I. G. Baker Company manager at Macleod, the famous Howell Harris; Ezra Pearson, later of Medicine Hat; John McKean of Lundbreck — these men and many others were the men on the Benton, Montana, to Macleod route.

The ox, once broken, was a powerful and dependable beast, sixteen of them, eight pairs, on two, three and even four wagons, moving as one unit, plodding between the head of navigation on the Missouri River at Fort Benton and Macleod at a rate seldom exceeding 1½ miles an hour; 30 wagons or so to a train; 10 strings of bull teams pulling an average of three wagons each — 160 oxen.

Where did all the oxen come from? At Fort Benton, the I. G. Baker Co. had large pastures. Big, aged, range cattle were bought, matched for size, the pair yoked together, the yoke being hewn from hardwood, and a steel clevis bolted and riveted through the top of the yoke. The steers were then turned loose; fastened together in this manner they learned to walk in perfect unison. They fed, drank and lay down together, in time becoming as one. Green teams were tied in the centre of old and seasoned strings.

All big outfits had bull whackers, men who rode horseback, keeping the laggards and lazy oxen up on the yoke, pulling their weight. Bull whackers of that day were tough, honest and somewhat profane. They all had the knack of handling long bull whips, cracking them in the air over the backs of the oxen like the sound of a pistol.

At night camp, the wagons drew in, camped in a circle, the oxen turned loose, in pairs, under the watchful eye of the night wrangler.

Miles of these ox teams trailed across the prairies, in the '70s and '80s from Fort Benton, from Winnipeg to Edmonton, all bringing food and equipment, all recording another page in the building of the West.

Rider Davis of Fort Macleod, the son of D. W. Davis, told me that in Fort Benton today, a town of 1,500, still stands the large brick building used by the I. G. Baker Co. as a supply depot, a large painted sign across the top of the building, advertising the firm's name, is still in perfect condition.

CHAPTER 23
An Exciting Evening

One of the most eventful nights in the history of Calgary occurred Feb. 16, 1916.

During the First World War the feeling against Germans was intense. In Calgary large numbers of men were in training at Sarcee and Victoria Park.

The evening of which I speak, a mob of more than 500, mostly soldiers, wrecked the White Lunch at 128 - 8th Ave. E. The mob smashed the contents of the building completely — even tore the tile from the walls.

Above the restaurant was a dance hall run by a good Scot named McLellan which suffered the same fate. The reason given for the riot was that the manager of the White Lunch, Frank H. Nagel, had discharged a returned soldier and employed an Austrian in his place. It was brought out later that Mr. Nagel was not to blame.

The same night the mob went from there to the branch restaurant of the same company at 108 - 9th Ave. W. for a repeat performance. The police were powerless and it was not until General George Cruickshanks appeared on the scene and appealed to the men to return to their barracks, that the raiding stopped.

The following evening, however, the mob was again on the warpath and within 20 minutes wrecked the Riverside Hotel which stood just across the Langevin bridge. I vividly remember that evening. Four or five of the soldiers had been arrested and placed in the RCMP barracks, which at that time was located in the old Court House building on 4th St. W.

I was in a car watching the soldiers who were determined to raid the police barracks to release their comrades. There were some shots fired and one of the soldiers was wounded. They ran to my car, placed the wounded soldier in it, and away we went down 8th Ave. to the doctor's — soldiers standing on each side of the running board, shouting "gangway."

For weeks following these riots, patrols were placed at all central places of business, but there was no further trouble.

Edgar Lougheed, son of Sir James Lougheed, told me that on the same occasion, the building superintendent of the Lougheed Building, Jimmy Hunter, was anxious about Cronn's Rathskeller, the restaurant in the basement.

With great presence of mind, he called a truck to cut the wires leading to the large sign that hung outside advertising "Cronn's" and to cart it away; turned out all lights; and locked the doors to the building. The restaurant was not touched; but Mr. Lougheed tells me that Mr. and Mrs. Cronn disappeared that night and he never afterwards heard of their whereabouts.

CHAPTER 24
Calgary Exhibition and Stampede

The Calgary Agricultural Society dates back to 1884 when Col. James Walker arranged with A. M. Burgess, then a deputy minister of the interior, for a grant of land, now known as Victoria Park, 94 acres, for the sum of $235, with a proviso that the site was to be used thereafter for exhibition purposes only.

In 1900 the Calgary Agricultural Society was reorganized as the Inter-Western Pacific Exhibition Co. Ltd. In 1911 the name was changed to the Calgary Industrial Exhibition and in 1933 to the name, now world famous, the Calgary Exhibition and Stampede. During the years many well-know Calgarians, hundreds, in fact, have faithfully served on the directorate of the exhibition.

Through the years Calgary businessmen have devoted their time and efforts, making the Calgary Exhibition the worldwide success, as we know it today.

The following is a list of the presidents and the years in which they served: 1884-85, Augustus Carney; 1886-87-92, Col. James Walker; 1888-91, Amos Rowe; 1893-94, Howard Douglas; 1895, James Reilly; 1896, R. G. Robinson; 1897-98, A. E. Cross; 1899-1900 and 1903, Col. A. J. Wolley-Dodd; 1901-1902, J. R. Sutherland; 1904, James Smart; 1905-1906, Osborne Brown; 1907-13, I. S. C. Van Wart; 1914-23, E. J. Dewey; 1924-25, Fred Johnston; 1926-32, N. J. Christie; 1933-36, C. M. Baker; 1937-40, J. Charles Yule; 1941-43, T. A. Hornibrook;

The first Calgary Stampede parade along 8th Ave., 1912.

The Pendleton cowboys' band at first Calgary Stampede, 1912.

1944-46, R. W. Ward; 1947-48, A. H. McGuire; 1949-51, Jas. B. Cross;

Since 1951 the presidents have been: 1952-53, George Edworthy; 1954-56, W. A. Crawford-Frost; 1957-59, F. Clar Manning; 1960-61, Merv. Dutton; 1962-63, H. Gordon Love; 1964-65, Donald C. Matthews; 1966-67, C. T. Baker.

In 1905, E. L. Richardson was appointed general manager, continuing until 1940 when J. Charles Yule — Charlie to thousands — took over.

The Stampede section of today's show presents the glamor that attracts thousands upon thousands to our city, but it must be remembered that the primary object is the exhibition, showing Southern Alberta's livestock, grain, produce, commerce and natural resources.

The aims of the Calgary Exhibition Board are as follows: To perpetuate the memory of the old timers; to promote livestock, through annual shows and sales; to display the development of nat-

ural resources and commerce; to promote sport in as many phases as possible; to perpetuate the life of the western cattleman, his activities, his work on the range, his sports (the Stampede) and furthering of rural and urban girl and boy activities, calf clubs, baking, dressmaking, etc.

It is interesting to trace the various activities of the exhibition through the years. May I give you the highlights of several annual shows? Dominion Exhibition 1908 (note the advertising of that day) "Visit Alberta before the golden opportunity, picturesque riders and the Indians are gone." Alberta Provincial Exhibition 1909, the famous Navassar Ladies' Band of New York. 1910, milking machine demonstration. 1911, Calgary Industrial Exhibition, Aeroplane, Mono Rail; 103rd Regimental Band. 1912, Jimmy Ward with his Curtiss airplane. 1913, Past and Present. 1914, Better Babies contest. 1915, Grand Military Program; fireworks 300 ft. long illustrating Forcing the Dardanelles. 1916, Greatest Loop the

Loop Aviator, Miss Katherine Stinson. 1917, Automobile Races. 1918, Forget your worries and keep fit; auto races, horse races. 1919, Passenger carrying airplanes, Capt. Fred McCall, Capt. Wop May; Sousa and his Band. 1920, Locklear, changing planes in mid-air; auto polo; 48th Highlanders Band. 1921, Fireworks display, 200 ft. reproduction The Naval Battle of Dover and the Thavius Band. 1925, the World's Longest Team, 36 horses and 10 wagons.

It must be said that the Calgary exhibition through the years pro-vided plenty of variety.

From the minutes of directors' meetings I gleaned the following: June 13, 1903. Moved that a large tent be erected for the directors facing the office door and that 2 doz. lager and 2 doz. ginger beer be provided. June 22, 1905. Moved that lager, scotch and rye whiskey, syphon, seltzer and ginger beer be provided for directors' rooms, and that J. R. Thompson be appointed to take charge of the directors' quarters. June 19, 1906. Moved that soft drinks and cigars only be provided for directors' quarters.

"The Big Four"

At Stampede time, the Calgary newcomer must wonder, "How did this world famous show start? Who were responsible?

To earlier Calgarians, their minds must go back to the days of 1912. With pride they remember four men of that day; four men who had faith in this city; faith to back up the ideas of a young cowboy — Guy Weadick — who with H. C. McMullen, the general livestock agent of the CPR, conceived the idea of a gigantic out-door western show.

George Lane, A. E. Cross, Patrick Burns and Hon. A. J. Mc-Lean, for years now known as the "Big Four", put up the necessary money. Westerners responded and on Sept. 2, 3, 4 and 5, 1912, put over the first Calgary Stampede, a financial success.

The show lasted only four days, but those four days were all-important to the future of Calgary. History was made those mild September days in 1912, the out-come of which has made this city of ours known around the world.

The 1912 Stampede was no mean affair. Early Calgarians will remember the seating arrangement,

bleachers clear around the mile track. One could write of the deeds of the "Big Four", of their success in the West, but let me mention only how Calgarians of that day sized them, and a quote from their biographies as printed in 1912.

Patrick Burns — "Modest, un-assuming and likeable. A keen business man; a lover of clean sport and a true friend. Few in this great west land have so firm a grip on the affections of the people as has our genial Pat Burns."

A. E. Cross — "A shrewd, prac-tical man of business. To his busi-ness and executive ability, and high standards of honor, as well as his keen devotion to what he considers his public duties, this province of Alberta owes a great deal."

George Lane — "With a vision that was almost uncanny he early foresaw the possibilities of the then unknown plains of the Northwest. A born optimist with unlimited faith in himself and a plain blunt way of presenting facts."

Hon. A. J. McLean — "He built up the export cattle trade to such a standard that the name of Archie

McLean was for 20 years synonymous with fair dealing and business integrity."

The showmanship and energy of Guy Weadick did much to perpetuate future stampedes.

E. L. Richardson and for ten years Charlie Yule, and men like Alex Hornibrook, R. W. Ward, Art McGuire, Jim Cross, George Edworthy, Dick Cosgrave, the late Jack Dillon and "Squibb" Ross and many others developed the show to its tremendous proportions that we know today.

The year 1919 saw the next Calgary Stampede, appropriately named "The Victory Stampede". In 1923 the first joint Exhibition and Stampede was held and since that day it has developed, until spectators find it necessary to buy their July tickets in January. The Calgary Stampede — the greatest show of its kind in the world.

CHAPTER 25

Sports and Sportsmen
"The Greatest Rider of Them All"

In the '90s the sports arena of this city was an open field situated where Victoria School is now located. A grandstand of sorts stood on the location of Pilkingtons Ltd. The field boasted a track of about a quarter mile in length.

The big sports event of the year was the voluntary firemen's celebration of the 24th of May.

Old timers tell me there were some interesting characters in those days. One was a man whom they called Douker, a great horseman, whose favorite sport was riding Roman style astride two horses at full gallop. He was an excellent shot with a pistol, and it is said that the walls of his bachelor shack at Pine Creek (near Midnapore) were punctured with holes— every night he shot out the candle flame for practice.

Then there were the Marshall boys, Lee and Tiny, who always performed on sports day. Lee would hold a bunch of flowers at arm's length while Tiny, coming on horseback at full gallop, would cut the tops off the flowers with one crack of a long bull whip. The Marshall boys worked for R. G. Robinson on the Chipman Ranch. Lee was later killed in the United States where he was a professional rider.

Then, in those days the firemen promoted Indian races which were far different from those of today. The young braves rode naked, except for a breach cloth, and bareback of course, because no Indian ever needed a saddle.

There was Jim Touhey, a rider who later worked for the P. Burns ranches. But, I want to mention the horse he loved best, a buckskin (today he would be given the fancy name of Palomino). Jim called his pony "Six Bits" because that is what he paid for him—75 cents. Across from the City Hall was a livery stable which was torn down a few years ago, and on the side of the barn someone had painted the picture of a horse—that picture was of "Six Bits". Jim and "Six Bits" could always be found at the May 24 sports day events.

The greatest rider of them all was a successful rancher by the name of John Ware. I well remember John Ware, a Negro, being spoken of as one of the "whitest" men in the West. He was liked by everyone of that day, and associated freely with the best of them.

He was a man of tremendous strength and could conquer the wildest of horses. Thousands of businessmen were served by his son, Bob Ware. who for years was a Pullman porter on the midnight train to Edmonton.

Polo In Elbow Park

Calgary played polo in the early days — expertly too. In fact some of Calgary's best players were rated as the finest.

The polo grounds in Calgary's early history was Elbow Park — the infield was what was then known as the Brigg's Race Track. This race track was really two tracks — one mile of it was inside track, and the outside mile and a quarter track was used for hurdle racing. One track ran into the other at the starting gate.

Frank (Bull) McHugh, a pioneer son born in Calgary in 1885, tells me that in 1904 T. S. C. Lee offered the McHugh family the 140 acres including the race track which is now known as Elbow Park, for $5,000 — $1,000 cash. But, as "Bull" McHugh says, in those days it was open prairie except for the race track — why buy it! The McHughs used it for pasture anyway — for free!

About 1906 the property was sold to F. C. Lowes, but the boys continued to play polo in the enclosure until some time after Freddy Lowes bought the property.

One morning Major Collin Ross and "Bull" McHugh went out for practice. "My word," said the major, an Englishman "we can't play polo here.. The horses will fall and break their necks." Surveyors had taken over and survey stakes were sticking up all over. "No, major," said Bull, "we can't play today, but let's play tomorrow."

During the night the survey stakes mysteriously disappeared. The boys continued to play polo for several days, until Freddy Lowes came out to check his surveying.

According to another story that "Bull" tells: In 1907 Major Ross, Justin Dean-Freeman, a fellow by the name of Barrett, and "Bull" McHugh, all made a deal to play polo in California at Del Coronado Beach. The horses were to be shipped from Calgary. The major, Dean-Freeman and McHugh all turned up; but where was Barrett? As time went on they couldn't imagine what had happened to him, until about a month later the major received a wire relayed from Calgary — "Where are you fellows and the horses." Barrett had landed in England. Mr. McHugh says there may have been an excuse for Barrett misunderstanding the instructions as for over a week before they left, they all were in a perpetual daze.

The first golf course in Calgary was located where the Al Azhar Temple stands today.

About 1903 the little frame golf house was moved to Elbow Park — it stood where the Messenger home is today on Sifton.

After Elbow Park was subdivided, the Country Club obtained its present location.

Baseball

Calgary was a great baseball town in the early years of this century. In the years 1907 to 1912 and again in 1920 to 1923 Calgarians enjoyed professional class "B" baseball.

As early as 1905 the Alberta Amateur League had been formed among Edmonton, Wetaskiwin, Olds, Medicine Hat, Banff, and Anthracite. Baseball was played in Victoria Park. A well known citizen, Alf McLean, was the "mascot" of the 1905 amatuer team.

From memory he gave me the line-up, Fred Adams, the hotel manager, was president; Sam Giles the manager, Ralph Corbett the captain.

The players were Gordon Connell, Jimmy Heisler, George Andrews, William Kirkham, William Irvine, Fred Tarrant, Lew Winkler, Horace Steadman, Bill Connelly, Leo Deaver, and Leo Howard.

Sunday ball was played in 1905 by another city league—"The Bartenders" "The Barbers" and "The Fire Department."

The ball diamond was in Moccasin Flats near Irish Mellon's Blue Rock Hotel. The boys in the league were going fine until one sad day. One Sunday as usual the game was being played and a chap by the name of Charley Plemisser hit a fast ball.

Unfortunately a funeral procession was going by at that exact moment. The ball sailed right through the plate glass window of the Graham and Buscomb's hearse. That was just a little too much for Calgary citizens and the town council ruled Sunday ball "out."

In 1907 professional ball was organized with the Western Canada League comprising Edmonton, Lethbridge, Medicine Hat and Calgary. The line-up of the Calgary 1907 team was as follows: Russell, Taylor, O'Neil, O'Donnell, Chandler, Farrell, Shine, Quinn, Barrett, Barnstead and Driscoll.

In 1909 appears the names of Fred Lepper, Rochon, Baker, Parkes, Strandridge, Lloyd Turner, Pop Gouchie, and Jansen. In that year Winnipeg, Moose Jaw, Brandon and Regina joined the league.

Charlie Crist pitched for Edmonton and one season later joined the Calgary team.

Jimmy Flannagan, Wally Smith, and Sammy Vivien also played for Calgary in 1909. The field was called the Savage field situated in Victoria Park, Sam Savage being the president of the Calgary club.

In 1911, Andy and Henry Baxter played on the Edmonton team.

In 1920 baseball was re-organized. Dr. J. H. Birch was the president. A famous baseball umpire "Beans" Reardon, umpire-in-chief of the National League, started his baseball career in this town in 1920. Thousands remember his rasping "You're OUT."

Then in 1908 Calgary had a commercial league that played ball on the corner of 19th Ave. and 4th St. W. The Rev. Bob Pearson, Harry Ballentyne of the YMCA, Dan Lucy (3rd base for the Liberals), Stan Horne, Gordon Love and Guy Morton were a few of the players.

Let's finish these rambling remarks with Calgary's baseball story "It's true."

In 1911 Calgary and Edmonton were in the playoffs. Calgary's three pitchers were in a bad way —they needed a rest, whilst Edmonton's flinging staff was in top form and raring to go. The evening before the final game heavy black clouds came up, Calgarians were jubilant. "It was going to rain."

The game would be called. But the rain clouds blew over and the game-saving moisture passed by. However, at noon next day word was sent out—no game— the diamond is a quagmire.

The Edmonton manager, Deacon White, was wild, but after examining the field he swearingly agreed that the game couldn't be played. What aroused his suspicions was the marks of a garden hose in the mud.

The Calgary team pleaded innocent. Wild Bill Carney, the manager, claimed his boys were all in bed before nine.

Calgary was half a game ahead in the schedule and had the game been played and won by Edmonton, Edmonton would have captured the pennant. That evening Bill Carney and Moose Baxter, an Edmonton former player and supporter, battled it out in front of "Chan's" Cigar Store. Edmonton won that.

Calgary's Most Famous Fight

In the fall of 1907, Jim Sewell stepped off the train in Calgary. For a number of years he had been in the clothing business in Chicago and Detroit. His friend, Noah Brusso, had told him: "Jim, you go out west, locate the best town. I'll raise the money in the east and we'll go into business together." Jim, in a matter of days said to himself, "this is it." He wired Brusso, and arranged to buy out the business of John Hanna, that beloved Calgarian who for years was the secretary of the Calgary Board of Trade.

The night Jim's friend came to Calgary, Jim had a band out to meet him. Jim didn't have much trouble persuading the band, for you see the friend they were meeting was the heavyweight champion of the world, Tommy Burns (Noah Brusso). Tommy liked Jim's choice of a town and here he stayed.

Jim Sewell soon arranged an exhibition bout in the Sherman Rink. Tommy Burns agreed to spar with Jake Fullerton and Billy Lauder before a packed house.

Tommy Burns won the world's championship by defeating Marvin Hart in Los Angeles and after many fights, some of them in the British Isles, lost to Jack Johnson, whom he fought in Melbourne, Australia. The police stopped the fight in the 14th round, but not before Tommy Burns had broken three of Johnson's ribs.

On May 24, 1913, Tommy Burns promoted the most famous fight ever held in Calgary. In an arena built in the Manchester subdivision, Arthur Pelkey fought Luther McCarty. Tommy Burns was Pelkey's manager and the famous sports writer, Bill McCarney of The Chicago Tribune managed McCarty. The sports editor of The Chicago American was the referee.

But let Jim Sewell tell the story: Pelkey's headquarters were at the well-known hotel, the Blue Rock. McCarty located at the National Hotel in East Calgary. McCarty was a big, fine looking youngster, crazy about horses and cowboys, even dressing the part. Two days before the fight, McCarty, while riding was thrown, injuring his neck. But the fight went on as scheduled.

Personally I had a ticket to the fight but didn't see it. There weren't many cars in those days and my cousin, George McNeill, and I were doing pretty good driving fellows to the fight. We made one too many trips, and when we finally arrived the fight was disastrously over.

According to Jim Sewell, Pelkey and McCarty were called for the first round. They took up a sparring position, but before a hard blow was thrown, McCarty's head snapped back and he fell to the canvas. Fifteen doctors worked over him but in a matter of a few minutes he was dead.

Pelkey left the ring not knowing McCarty had died. He and Tommy Burns returned to the latter's home, where Pelkey had dressed for the fight. The coroner's jury gave their decision that the death was accidental. A popular young fellow by the name of "Sport" Smith was the lawyer handling Burns' and Pelkey's affairs, none other than A. L. Smith, K.C., M.P.

Lloyd Turner

I have told about the world's boxing champion, Tommy Burns, how he came here and lived here for six or seven dramatic years.

There is another Calgarian who, for more than 50 years, day in and day out, in his quiet unassuming way, did more to promote sport in this city than any other individual. He is a lover of clean sport and a friend to all. He is the man who, in 1945, took over the management of the Stampeder hockey team when they were in the doldrums, and in the matter of weeks, helped organize the team so thoroughly, that when the season closed, the team was victorious in the finals for the senior amateur title of Canada, the Allan Cup. Who is he? Lloyd Turner. His team also was in the Allan Cup finals in 1948 and 1950.

Lloyd Turner came to this city in 1910 as a professional ball player — a catcher with the old Western Canada League (Edmonton - Lethbridge - Calgary - Medicine Hat). He was born in Elmvale, Ontario, but was no stranger to Calgary, as his father, James Turner, was a contractor here.

After baseball was through in 1910, Lloyd Turner became associated with Bill Sherman, and for years managed the old Sherman Rink in this city's early days. For years he was manager of the Victoria Arena, and then the Corral.

Early Calgary baseball fans will remember the days when Lloyd Turner managed the Hillhurst Hustlers. Hockey enthusiasts will recall that four winters he managed the Minneapolis Millers, and

The Sherman Rink destroyed by fire, 1915.

for two years the Seattle Mets. His friend Josh Henthorn told me that when Lloyd Turner and he went to Minneapolis, the city there boasted only five hockey teams. In four years, Lloyd's enthusiasm for hockey, his leadership and organizing ability, had developed hockey to such an extent that 300 hockey teams were organized — principally school teams.

In his quiet way, Lloyd Turner is responsible for the popularity of sport in this city. The youth of Calgary owes him a great merit of thanks.

CHAPTER 26
"The Good Old Days"

L. V. Kelly (who was a Calgary Herald reporter, 1906-1916) in his well-known book, "The Range Men," tells this story. The financial backers of the Oxley Ranch were Alexander Staveley Hill and Lord Lathom, lord high chamberlain to Queen Victoria. During the summer of 1895 the above gentlemen visited the West.

While here they had lunch in the well-known eating house at Macleod at that time run by the famous old timer, Kamouse Taylor. Kamouse, a man with varied experiences from preacher to whisky trader, to squaw man, was greatly impressed with the honor of feeding such distinguished guests.

He personally undertook to serve the guests. Throwing a dirty towel over his forearm, he approached, saying to Mr. Hill: "Soup?" Mr. Hill would take soup.

Taylor, flourishing the towel gracefully, then approached Lord Lathom. "Soup?" Being British to the core, Lord Lathom wanted to know what was going to be the result before he committed himself. So, turning in his naturally dignified way, he asked: "What kind of soup?"

Taylor, essentially western and perhaps a bit flustered, too, replied with strong emphasis: "Damn good soup, yer lordship."

Not understanding the "queer" ways of the west, Lord Lathom looked at Kamouse Taylor with deep astonishment.

* * *

Surprising as it may seem to our present generation, I remember as a boy listening to Rev. Dr. George W. Kerby preach his sermons on Sunday evenings over the telephone.

Dr. Kerby, long before radio was invented, brought his message into early Calgary homes in this unique manner. He had an arrangement with the Bell Telephone Co. to connect any town phone up with a telephone that he spoke into from the pulpit of Central Methodist Church. Many a Sunday evening I listened to Dr. Kerby's message glued to the telephone receiver.

As I look back to those early days, I must confess the possible reason I listened so intently was the fact it kept me from being put to bed.

* * *

The early 1900's saw the heydey of the minstrel shows, burlesque, ragtime and early vaudeville.

About this time, too, the first phonographs were introduced, with an old favorite for 1897, "Don't Give Up the Old Love for the New," among the first recordings, as were "Sweet Rosie O'Grady," "Whisper Your Mother's Name," "On the Mississippi" and "There'll Be a Hot Time in the Old Town Tonight."

* * *

My uncle George Frazer in 1884 operated a confectionery and baking business. During the "Scott Act Period" — prohibition — apples, grapes, etc., were brought into the country in large lugs. Of course, it wouldn't have paid if there hadn't been a joker to the shipments. In the centre of the lugs was always a small keg of whisky.

One shipment contained an especially large bunch of Ontario

grapes. George Frazer put the grapes in the window. Soon in walked a Mountie who had been on patrol duty for weeks. "How much for the grapes?" said he. George, sizing the situation up, said: "$5." The Mountie paid the $5, an unheard of price, and walking out ate the grapes out of his hand.

In 1905 Calgary's leading hotels advertised their prices: $1.50 to $2 per day, "American plan."

Electric lighting for homes was introduced in Calgary in 1889. The power plant was the fifth in the Dominion.

Shagganappi — a well-known Calgary district — is an Indian name meaning rawhide.

George Murdoch — The first mayor of Calgary — named his son Calgary Murdoch.

An advertisement by a local clothing company appearing in 1907, featured men's beaver coats $42.50; men's first quality coon fur coats $25.

One of Calgary's best known old timers was Romeo Miquelon who operated a large liquor shop. According to today's standards, the price of liquor was fantastic. The best Scotch procurable cost $1.25 for a 40 oz. bottle overproof, unwatered by any government agencies.

Yet there wasn't as much drunkenness as today. Liquor was cheap, easily procured and used by the old timer with precaution.

Romeo was a great fellow, a friend of all. One day Romeo received a shipment of rare French wines. Romeo decorated his window appropriately, placing the rare wine in a prominent position in the window with a large sign announcing the price — $5 a bottle. Romeo didn't immediately sell his treasure but he had plenty of interested spectators. "Romeo, you're crazy," "Who ever heard of wine worth $5 a bottle?" Romeo caused a sensation. History does not record who bought the precious nectar.

To discourage settlers from moving to Western Canada, traders in the early days spread the story that west of Portage la Prairie the ground never thawed out and wheat could not be grown.

The annual licence fee for restaurants in 1920 was $1.

In prohibition days under the Scott Act, an early Calgarian taxidermist had a famous "stuffed coyote."

To the thirsty population of those early days this stuffed coyote had a peculiar attraction. By a remarkable coincidence one could lift the head of the "coyote", hold a cup at a predetermined spot at the rear of the stuffed animal and get a "drink." Of course you paid to put your hand under his chin.

In 1918 Calgary had 74 passenger cars and six trailer cars operating over 75 miles of transit railway track and carrying nearly 17,000,000 paying passengers.

The following "society" item appeared in an early issue of The Calgary Herald before the turn of the century.

Our gent's underwear in scarlet and grey at $2 a suit is the best ever offered at the price.

The I. G. Baker Company, operating Calgary's first store, used I. G. Baker money to trade with the Indians — a brass token about the size of a silver dollar was used, bearing the simple inscription:

I. G. Baker and Co. $1.00.

In The Calgary Herald of Dec. 15, 1909, a well-known department store advertised the following Christmas hampers: 9 lb. turkey, 2 lb. plum pudding, 2 lbs. cranberries, 2 lbs. mincemeat, 2 lbs. raisins, 1 lb. nuts, 1 lb. figs, 2 lbs. candy, 2 cans tomatoes, peas and corn, 1 lb. Huntley and Palmer biscuits, 1 lb. grapes, 2 lbs. Tetley's tea, 1 lb. coffee, 3 bottles pickles, 14 oz. bottle each of the following: port, sherry, brandy, Scotch, claret. Total price—$13.25.

One imperial quart bottle each of the following: brandy, claret, port, Old Rye, sherry, Scotch. Price—$4.00.

School attendance in Calgary in 1908 was 2,980 pupils attending 58 schools.

CHAPTER 27

The Spirit of Calgary

My friend Harry Hutchcroft in these few verses wrote what I have been trying to say.

Thanks, Harry, for letting me quote you.

THE SPIRIT OF CALGARY
by Harry Hutchcroft

Written and dedicated to the Southern Alberta Pioneers and presented by the writer at a citizens' banquet in honor of the late Senator Patrick Burns on the occasion of his 75th birthday.

Say neighbor, here's something that I'd like to know;
It's something I'm trying to answer and so
I'm wondering if you can help me at all.
But maybe you'll think it's too trifling and small,
I'll admit it's long been quite a poser to me—
Why is it most everyone loves Calgary?

And why is it when fate takes you
  far away,
Your heart ever yearns to return
  there someday?
And why does the glimpse of a
  Calgary face
Make you homesick and wish you
  could see the old place?
Once again I'll admit it's a teaser
  to me
Why a fellow gets lonesome for
  old Calgary.

I wonder just what the attraction
  can be!
I wonder what makes it so precious to me!
Can it be the bright sunshine we
  get every day?
Can it be that I know just a few
  miles away
Rise those wonderful Rockies
  a'callin' to me
That makes me just long for my
  old Calgary.

Can it be the green foothills sur-
  rounding us here,
Or the Bow and the Elbow with
  waters so clear?
It may be. I guess it's got some-
  thing to do
With the fact that without them
  I'm lonesome and blue.
But it seems that there's some-
  thing that one cannot see
Makes most of us cherish the word
  "Calgary".

Yes, I'm sort of deciding, (just in
  my own mind)
That this something or other
  I've mentioned we'll find,
Is the PIONEER SPIRIT of long,
  long ago,
When the doors had no locks and
  wherever we'd go
We were welcome, yes, as welcome
  as could be,
And that spirit still lingers in old
  Calgary.

It's slipping away with the passing
  of years,
They're crowding it out with their
  modern ideas.
They're letting their so-called "Society Chart"
Gauge a man by his dollars and
  not by his heart.
So it's something for which mighty
  glad we should be
There's a wee bit still with us in
  old Calgary.

So treasure it friend, through the
  forthcoming years,
And honor the memory of those
  pioneers
Like Burns, Lane and Cross and
  others we hail
As leaders who years ago blazoned
  a trail
And conceived a spirit that men
  now agree
Is the wonderful SPIRIT OF OLD
  CALGARY.

CHAPTER 28
Banff the Beautiful
Dr. R. G. Brett

Banff the Beautiful! How fortunate Calgarians are to be only 77 miles away.

When the CPR was constructed through the mountains in 1883-85, the Canadian government wisely decided that Banff belonged to the people of Canada. From that time to the present, no individual has ever had an outright title to property in Banff. All property is controlled by the parks department by long-term leases.

Many pioneer men have claimed that they discovered the famous hot springs, but it will suffice to describe what they actually found in those early days.

There was no tunnel to the cave of the Cave and Basin as it is known today; this was cut through for convenience. The entrance to this cave was through the small hole at the top and down a ladder. Many old timers will recall going down this ladder to bath in the pool. I have been told that when the cave was first discovered, the ceiling was covered with beautiful stalactites, which were, one by one, broken off and caried away for souvenirs.

The CPR soon realized the value of Banff and, in 1886, built a small hotel on the present site of the Banff Springs Hotel. Credit is due to CPR officials of that day for the splendid location they chose.

One of the unique characters of Banff before 1910, was a wonderful Scot by the name of D. D. Galletley. He was an institution in himself. As caretaker of the Cave and Basin, dressed in kilts, he presided over his domain with all the dignity of a Scottish chieftain. To have him conduct a party through the Cave was impressive, to say the least; and believe me he really kept us youngsters in order.

The horse-drawn tally-ho was the only mode of transportation permitted in Banff. As late as 1913, cars were barely tolerated, and it was the rule of the park that all automobiles entering the park go directly to their destination, to be parked until departure. Later, one-way traffic was introduced, with a speed limit of 10 miles an hour, and a ruling to stop when horse-drawn vehicles approached.

The Brewster family has been in the transportation business in Banff since 1888.

Another old timer to Banff was Hon. Dr. Robert G. Brett, who established the Banff Sanatorium in 1886 on the present site of the government buildings. In 1909, he established the Banff Hospital. Dr. Brett was appointed lieutenant-governor of Alberta in 1915.

Old timers tell this story about Dr. Brett. When he was the lieutenant-governor, he took a trip in a private railway car up to Fort George. One old trapper in the district heard of the lieutenant-governor coming to town and, never having seen a governor, he decided he would like to meet this great man. So he hiked in to the railway and on asking where he could see the governor, was told to go right into his private car. On coming out, someone said, "Well, Bill, did you see the lieutenant-governor?"

"Hell no," replied Bill, "there's no one in there except 'Old Doc Brett'."

Banff's Old Timers

Banff, in 1902, boasted a population of 250 people.

The park superintendent was Howard H. Douglas, an old-time westerner, who first came to Calgary in 1882 where he was in charge of all CPR supplies between Brandon, Manitoba, and Revelstoke, B.C. From 1884-96 he and Mr. Stirrett ran a cartage business here.

Then, in 1896, Mr. Douglas was appointed park superintendent at Banff, staying until 1910, when he moved to Edmonton as commissioner of all Dominion parks. In later years he became the chief motion picture censor for the province.

In 1902, the boat-house on the Bow River at Banff was operated by William Mather.

Dave White operated his general store in the same location as his son ran the business after him.

One of Banff's most interesting old timers was Tom Wilson, a guide and general outfitter, who in 1882 discovered one of the beauty spots of the world — Lake Louise.

The postmaster was G. M. Fears, who, with his brother, also operated the first curiosity shop for tourists.

W. L. Matthews was the manager of the Banff Springs Hotel. Frank Beattie operated the Park Hotel. The Alberta Hotel was operated by Frank Ricks and W. J. Potts. E. M. Peyto was a mountain guide.

One of Banff's most colorful old timers was Norman K. Luxton, at one time business manager for The Calgary Herald. What an adventurous fellow he was in his youth. I'll tell you about just one of his escapades. In 1899, with Captain John Voss as his only companion, Mr. Luxton made a trip across the Pacific Ocean in the "Tilikum", a trim little boat fashioned from a red cedar log, which had a 28-foot keel and a capacity of 2½ tons. Mr. Luxton and the captain visited 42 islands and covered 14,000 miles. Mr. Luxton's wife, Georgina, was David McDougall's daughter.

From 1906 to 1914 Calgarians got plenty of excitement just by taking a motor trip to Banff.

I remember, about 1909, the newly formed AMA organized a caravan to make the trip. I have a photo that shows about a dozen cars (practically every car the city boasted) lined up on 7th Ave. — ready to go. In the lead was the pilot car, and coming up at the rear was a trouble car loaded with extra gasoline, extra parts, tires, pumps and chains.

Julien Chatel was in charge of this car. In one of the other cars was P. D. Sprung and his family. It was one of the sorrows of my youth that I was not invited to go along. Mr. Sprung's car was an "E.M.F.". "E.M.F." stood for "E. M. Flanders", one of the founders of Studebaker.

The caravan started out early in the morning, and most of them arrived at Banff late that evening. A few cars fell by the wayside.

The following year Albert Denby, who was Mr. Sprung's partner in the Western Tent and Awning Co., bought a car that was called the "Apperson Jackrabbit."

That summer, the Sprungs and the Denbys decided again to make the hazardous trip to Banff. This time I was lucky, for they invited me along. We left early in the morning and at about 2 o'clock reached the Anthracite Hill. The "Jackrabbit" refused to make it and, with a sickening sigh stopped, half way up. We did not need to worry about traffic, so we blocked the wheels, got out the lunch basket and ate.

After lunch we had a conference on how to get the "Jackrabbit" up the hill. Someone thought it might be an idea to blow into the gas tank at the rear of the car. We blew; one of the men cranked; and, with a fitful cough, the car started.

Mr. Sprung always says we "blew the car up the hill." Actually we did, for while Albert Denby steered, we took turns running behind, blowing into the tank.

In those days cars were not built for mountain driving; the gas tank was placed at a lower level than the front end, and the "Jackrabbit" ran like the wind on the level, but was no mountain sheep.

Banff in 1884

Canmore's Famed Author

The second Sunday in September of 1927 was one of those clear crisp autumn days that beautiful Banff often produces. The roads and pathways were thronged with cars and people wending their way out past the golf course to a natural amphitheatre known as the Devil's Cauldron.

The Highland games had been played for the last three days and today was the finale — a Highland outdoor church service. By 3 o'clock, the time arranged for the service, thousands had gathered on the banks of the cauldron. Suddenly, down in the centre of the "bowl," there appeared a minister dressed in his colorful Cameron Highlander's costume, escorted by Scottish pipers playing beloved Scottish airs.

The crowd was hushed and reverent when Rev. Dr. C. W. Gordon began the service. Scottish hymns were sung to the accompaniment of the pipes. Dr. Gordon, who was no stranger to the land, for he had been the minister at the little Canmore church nearby, delivered a sermon appropriate to the West.

He had been ordained in Calgary in 1890 and had spent years in the West, living the life of a sacrificing churchman, roughing it in lumber camps and in poor parishes.

Dr. Gordon was the minister of the Canmore Presbyterian Church in 1888. Shortly after the arrival of a new family to the town, he was requested to baptize their child. The baptism was to take place at the Sunday evening church service. The announcement that afternoon was the signal for a gala celebration.

Arriving at the church that evening long before the minister, who was frequently late because he had to ride in eight miles from Anthra-cite where he held an afternoon service, they decided that a dance would be most fitting for the joyous occasion. So the floor of the little church was cleared — the seats were easily disposed of, as they were only a few planks on nail kegs.

When Dr. Gordon finally arrived, the fiddler was on the platform by the pulpit, the dance was in full swing and Scotch whisky was flowing freely. Instead of trying to stop them with a show of disapproval, Dr. Gordon hit upon the idea of announcing a hymn during intermission. He soon had the affair under control, but it was 1 a.m. before the baptismal service could be held.

This story exemplifies Dr. Gordon's ability to cope with an unusual situation.

But, back to Banff! Why did thousands go to that outdoor church service at the Cauldron? Many of them came from Calgary. It was to see and hear Dr. Gordon, better known to us as the famous Canadian author Ralph Connor.

CHAPTER 29
Origin of Alberta Town Names

Through the assistance of J. C. Jones, general superintendent of the CPR at Calgary, I was able to obtain some interesting information on the origins of names of CPR stations throughout this district. It would be impractical to record the names of all the stations, as there are 537 in the Alberta division, but I will list a few.

The history of these names is recorded as to the date the station was named.

Okotoks for example, is an Indian word meaning "Stony Cross-ing". Gull Lake is the translation of the Indian name "Kiaskus". Piapot was a self-made Indian chief living in the vicinity of Cypress Hills. Maple Creek was a nearby creek which got its name from the Manitoba maple trees which grew on its banks.

Mackid was named after H. G. Mackid, the first chief surgeon of the CPR in Calgary. Walsh was named after Major Walsh of the North West Mounted Police, of 1874. Irvine after Col. Irvine of the NWMP and later warden of the Manitoba penitentiary. Dunmore was named when Lord Dunmore made the trip to what was then the end of the steel.

Medicine Hat came from the translation of the Blackfoot Indian name of the place "Saamis" which meant headdress of medicine man. Cousins was named after William Cousins, a prominent old-time businessman of Medicine Hat. Redcliff was so called because of the red color of the cliffs on the river bank. Stair—from Stair Ranching Co. Suffield—after Lord Suffield. Tilley—after Sir Leonard Tilley. Brooks—after N. E. Brooks, former divisional engineer of the CPR. Cassils—after a prominent Montreal broker of that name. Southesk—named by the Earl of Southesk who crossed the prairie in the early days. Lathom—after the Earl of Lathom, prominent shareholder in Oxley Ranch.

Bassano was called after a character in the operetta "Merchant of Venice". Crowfoot—after a famous chief of the Blackfoot tribe. Cluny—after Cluny McPherson Stades when the railway was constructed there. Gleichen—after Count Gleichen, a prominent German bondholder of the CPR.

Barstow was named by the F. W. Stobart & Co., early traders in the Northwest, who reversed the name of the company, changing Stobart to Barstow. Indus — an Indian word meaning "constellation of the stars". Ogden was named after I. G. Ogden, financial vice-president of the CPR in Montreal. Alyth—the name of the first white child born in Calgary. Namaka is an Indian name meaning "The place of gun or bow". Strathmore—meaning "The Great Valley" or the most extensive plain.

Cheadle—after Dr. Cheadle of Milton & Cheadle, explorers. Langdon and Shepard were named after contractors who built the main line in that locality. Cantour was

the signature used by the Archbishop of Canterbury. Leader—the name was changed from "Prussia" during the First Great War. Estuary—the junction of the North and South Saskatchewan Rivers. Empress—in memory of Queen Victoria, Empress of India. Bindloss—after the poet Harold Bindloss. Cavendish—after Lady Cavendish and the family name of the Duke of Devonshire. Jenner—by Dr. Ed Jenner, famous surgeon-discoverer of vaccination. Iddesleigh—by the Earl of Iddesleigh. Patricia—after Princess Patricia, daughter of the Duke and Duchess of Connaught.

Rosemary was named for Rose and Mary, daughters of Earl Grey. Makepeace — William Makepeace Thackeray, author. Hussar—a German colony whose men had served in a regiment of the hussars. Standard—from the royal standard. Tudor—from the House of Tudor. Irricana—combination of irrigation and canal. Dalroy—combination of Dill & McElroy, local merchants. Keoma—an Indian name for "over there"—far away. Beiseker—after Senator Beiseker of North Dakota. Acme—Greek word meaning summit. When named it was the most northerly point on the CPR branch prior to 1909.

Gatine—in honor of Mrs. Gatine who boarded the construction crews in that district.

Kneehill came from Kneehill Creek that joins the Red Deer River there. Vauxhall—after the old gardens in London, England. Retlaw—the name Walter reversed; named after Walter R. Baker of Montreal. Schuler—name of a prominent farmer there. Hilda—first child born there. Seven Persons—the place where seven Blackfoot Indians were killed by the Assinaboines. Bow Island—the Indians came to an island in the

81

river there for wood for making bows. Taber—the first part of the word tabernacle, named by a Mormon settlement. Elcan—last part of the word tabernacle reversed. Barnwell — R. Barnwell, former general tie agent for the CPR. Chin—from the shape of a neighboring hill.

Lethbridge—after William Lethbridge, first president of North Western Coal & Navigation Co. Ltd. Kipp—from Fort Kipp—an old Indian trading post. Pearce—William Pearce of the DNR, Calgary. Brocket—Count Brocket of Derbyshire Hall, a former director of the CPR. Pincher Creek—in 1886 a party of prospectors lost a pair of pincers in the stream which were later found by the police.

Cowley — pasture land called "Cow-lea". Lundbreck— combination of two names, Lund & Breckenridge. Hillcrest—after Charles P. Hill, manager and director of Hillcrest Collieries. Frank — after H. L. Frank who opened the first coal mine in the Crowsnest Pass. Blairmore—after two former contractors, Blair and Moore. Coleman—after D. C. Coleman of the CPR. Crowsnest derived its name from Crowsnest Mountain, scene of a battle between the Crow and Blackfoot Indians.

Granum — a Latin name for grain. Claresholm—from Clare's Home, Mrs. J. Niblock's maiden name. Stavely—A. Staveley Hill, RCMP and former president of Oxley Ranch. Parkland—after an old-time resident, Park Hill. Nanton — Sir Augustus M. Nanton. Cayley — Mr. Cayley of Osler, Hammond, Nanton & Cayley.

High River—from the Highwood River. DeWinton—Major General Sir Francis DeWinton. Carmangay—C. W. Carman and wife Gay, former residents. Champion—from Alloway & Champion, private bankers of Winnipeg. Brant—a bird of that species. Cardston—Charles Ora Card, Morman founder of the town. Magrath—Charles A. Magrath. Raymond—Ray Knight, a rancher. Turin—after an imported Percheron stallion owned by a syndicate of farmers. Coutts—J. Burdett Coutts, a banker of London.

Shouldice—after James Shouldice. Crossfield—an engineer who was employed by C. & E. Carstairs—a town in Scotland. Didsbury—Jack Didsbury, C. & E. official. Olds—an officer of the same company, George Olds. Innisfail — a town in Ireland. Red Deer after the river of the same name.

Cochrane—the late Senator H. H. Cochrane. Morley—Rev. Morley Punshon, a Methodist minister. Seebe—an Indian name for river. Banff—named by Lord Strathcona after a town by that name in Scotland, his birthplace. Lake Louise —after Princess Louise. Hector—Dr. Hector of the Palliser expedition. Field—Cyrus West Field, a promoter of the Atlantic Cable Company, who visited the locality in 1884.

Ponoka — a Blackfoot Indian name for elk. Wetaskiwin—Indian for peace hills. Leduc—Father Leduc, 1865. Edmonton— Fort Edmonton, built in 1795. Stettler —Carl Stettler, a pioneer land land owner. Alix—Mrs. Alix Westhead, a pioneer rancher.

CHAPTER 30
History of Calgary, 1875 to 1967

By A. Parker Kent
(Associate Editor of The
Calgary Herald)

In August of 1875 a troop of 50 members of the NWMP, detached under command of Inspector A. E. Brisebois from the Macleod garrison, set up camp in the angle formed by the confluence of the Bow and Elbow rivers.

That was the beginning of Calgary as a settlement destined to become an important modern city. It was eight years after Canadian Confederation.

It was not the first time white men had set foot on this site. David Thompson, a Hudson's Bay Company trader, explorer and geographer, wintered with the Indians in this vicinity in 1787-88. He returned to explore the Bow River country again in 1800. One of his colleagues, Peter Fidler, spent the winter of 1793-94 with Peigan Indians near the present site of High River.

Other fur traders subsequently must have viewed this site. And in 1858 Captain John Palliser and his party of surveyors, appointed by the British government to find out what sort of country and climate existed west of Winnipeg, camped in the vicinity, perhaps at the very site where the NWMP raised their tents 17 years later.

The names of our two rivers, Bow and Elbow, represent translations from the Indian language. The Indians named the Bow River after trees along its upper valley which provided excellent wood for their shooting bows. Ma-na-cha-ban is the Cree name for Bow. The name Bow River appeared on a map drawn by English cartographer Arrowsmith as early as 1801. Mr. Arrowsmith likely got his information from David Thompson.

The Blackfoot word for Elbow is Mokin-tsis. That is what they called the winding river which enters the Bow after making a sharp, elbow-like turn near the Stampede grounds. As a matter of fact the Blackfoot still call Calgary Mokin-tsis. But the first white men here called the Elbow Swift Creek until they learned of its correct Indian designation.

Northwest Mounted Police Barracks in Calgary, about 1901.

When the police arrived they found two white settlers also encamped on the Elbow. One was Sam Livingston, an adventurous Irishman who had roamed and hunted up and down the western parts of North America and was on the verge of settling down to farming about where Chinook Park now is. The other settler was a missionary, Father Leon Doucet, who was doing missionary work among the Blackfoot.

After the police located here the missionary took up squatter's rights in what is now known as the Mission district of Calgary, and later Father Lacombe journeyed to Ottawa to have the property claim registered.

Before these things took place there had been an earlier event in the origin of the new settlement. Fred Kanouse, a colorful character who served the American Fur Company at its post named Fort Benton in Montana, briefly operated a crude post on the river bank in what is now Calgary's Elbow Park district. He built a log structure in 1871 and, with four other white men and an Indian women essayed to conduct trade with local Indians.

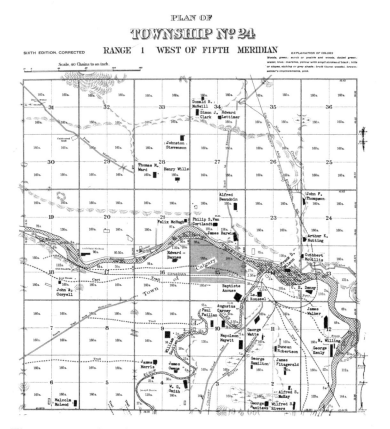

PLAN OF

TOWNSHIP Nº 24

SIXTH EDITION, CORRECTED   RANGE 1   WEST OF FIFTH MERIDIAN

The topographical survey map of township 24 in 1895, showing sections 14 (east Calgary) and 15 (CP's eventual townsite for Calgary), with homestead locations.

Sam Livingston

Following an incident between one of his men and a Blood Indian the neighboring Blood band attacked the post. For three days the traders kept the Indians at bay and a rescue party finally arrived from High River. Kanouse returned the next year but the struggle to become established was too great and he eventually located on the Oldman River.

Calgary likely was the scene of more than one Indian battle before the era of the white man. But history records one battle definitely, Kanouse's Battle of Elbow Park in which the whites stood off the hostiles for three days.

In 1875 it was still too early for supplies to come in by wagon train from Winnipeg; Fort Benton, Montana, was the supply station from the east. Boats brought freight to Fort Benton up the Missouri River. And the overland freight agency from Fort Benton was the I. G. Baker Company. It was to this firm that the NWMP turned for construction work and supplies when they reached Fort Macleod in 1874, and it was to this firm the new detachment on the Bow turned for help in 1875.

Two weeks after NWMP Inspector Brisebois' troop had arrived, two ox-drawn wagon outfits arrived at the new site carrying winter supplies for the troop and a working party to build a fort. Logs were cut upstream on the Elbow and floated down to the camp site. The Baker foreman was D. W. Davis who later became naturalized and a pioneer resident of the Macleod district and later a member of Parliament.

By November a log fort consisting of low buildings and surround-

Calgary's first town council in 1884: left to right, standing S. J. Hogg, Assessor J. Campbell, Solicitor Henry Bleecker, Dr. N. J. Lindsay, J. H. Millward, S. J. Clarke, Police Chief J. S. Ingram, Collector J. S. Douglas, I. S. Freeze; sitting Mayor George Murdoch, Treasurer Charles Sparrow, and Clerk T. T. A. Boys.

ing stockade had been erected. A cairn today marks the location of the fort. The Baker crew next constructed another 100-foot long building just south of the fort (across Ninth Ave.) to house an I. G. Baker store. And Calgary's first house was built nearby.

Mr. Davis stayed on a year as Baker store manager and was succeeded in 1877 by G. C. King. The fort served as the focal point of community interest for some time. It was the scene of socials and Saturday night dances and of Sunday church services.

In 1875 the Hudson's Bay Company had built a store on the east side of the Elbow River. The two trading companies competed until 1891 when the Baker firm sold out to the older and more traditional Canadian enterprise, the Hudson's Bay Company.

Meantime the name of Calgary had been given to the new settlement in the spring of 1876.

During the preceding winter Inspector Brisebois, who was in charge of the Mounted Police detachment which established the fort, decided all by himself that the new place should be called Fort Brisebois. After all, Fort Walsh and Fort Macleod had been named after NWMP officers. But when Fort Macleod's Major A. G. Irvine and NWMP Asst. Commissioner J. F. Macleod learned of Brisebois' decision they were greatly displeased. Col. Macleod suggested Calgary would be a better name, Calgarry being the name of an admirable property on Scotland's Isle of Mull, Col. Macleod's maternal ancestral home. It means clear running water. Officials in Ottawa concurred and the name was bestowed officially forthwith with one "r" being dropped along the way.

The names of Sam Livingston, who farmed first in the Elbow valley and later on the site of the Chinook polo ground, and John Glenn, who farmed at Midnapore in those earliest days, are perpetuated today in Heritage Park and the Horsemen's Hall of Fame, and by Glenmore Park and reservoir. The two men were the first to experiment with growing farm and garden products in the Calgary district.

With the Mounted Police fort established and Calgary now a place on the map, a sprinkling of white settlers began to come in. Herds of cattle and sheep were introduced and ranching commenced northward from Macleod to Cochrane. And wagon trips between Calgary and Winnipeg became more frequent.

It was not until the railway reached Calgary from Winnipeg in 1883, however, that the town really began to grow. The first train arrived on Aug. 28. It was two years before the CPR line was to reach Vancouver and three years before the first transcontinental train was to leave Montreal (June 28, 1886, with Sir John A. Macdonald on board) but a Dominion land office was opened and settlers began to come in.

By November of 1884 Calgary had a population of 500 and became incorporated as a town on Nov. 17. George Murdoch was elected the first mayor Dec. 3.

The first sawmill in Western Canada was built by Col. James Walker near Canmore in 1881 and this provided the growing town with lumber for its building needs until 1886 when some builders from Eau Claire, Wisc., brought sawmill machinery to Calgary and set up shop near the townsite. Logs for the Eau Claire Mills were floated down the Bow and brought down by train. The Eau Claire firm built the first traffic bridge over the Bow River near the present site of the Louise Bridge in 1887.

John Glenn

The year 1885, meanwhile, had been a busy and exciting one. The Riel rebellion posed a threat from neighboring Indians but an uprising did not materialize. Calgary's council asked for arms to protect itself, however. A combined town hall, police court and jail was built at a cost of $1,694. A hook-and-ladder fire brigade was organized. As the 1880s drew to a close the town of Calgary was a going concern and by 1893 was ready to become a city.

On Jan. 1, 1894, Calgary officially became a city. That was the date upon which its charter, signed a few weeks before by Hon. Charles H. Mackintosh, territorial lieutenant-governor, came into effect.

Elections were called immediately and W. F. Orr became the city's first mayor. He succeeded Alexander Lucas, last town mayor. Both had previously been editors of The Calgary Herald.

In 18½ years, from its beginnings as a Mounted Police fort, the first settlement in the Canadian Northwest to reach the status of cityhood had grown to have a population of 4,000 citizens.

The earlier years had seen great changes take place in the valley of the Bow, where the Elbow joins the larger stream. Tents and log buildings had been succeeded by houses built of sawn lumber and some, along with stores and commercial buildings, made of sandstone blocks.

The first big building to use sandstone was Knox Presbyterian Church, erected in 1887 at the intersection of streets now known as Centre St. and 7th Ave. The next year a court house was constructed of sandstone blocks, and it was torn down in 1958 to make way for the new court house which was completed in 1962.

One of the most notable of Calgary's early sandstone buildings

Calgary in 1889 at intersection of 8th Ave. and 1st St. S.W., looking east along 8th Ave. toward archway celebrating visit of Governor-General Lord Stanley.

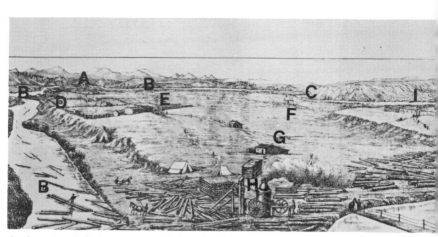

A sketch of Calgary in 1882, looking north down the Elbow River (B, in centre foreground), with the Bow (C, in background, at right). The NWMP's Fort Calgary (K) is depicted in left centre, while part of East Calgary, east of the Elbow, is shown in the sketch section at the right.

A panorama of Calgary in 1911, looking west over the Elbow, with 14th Ave. at the left, Downtown Calgary is

Identified in the drawing are: A, Roman Catholic Mission; B and C, Elbow and Bow; D, restaurant; E, I. G. Baker store; F, church; G and H, Cochrane range butcher shop and saw mill; K, Fort Calgary; L, boom bridge; M, Hudson's Bay; N, Capt. Denny's house.

shown curving from left background, toward right. The 2-storey building right foreground, was the General Hospital.

was the Alberta Hotel at the corner of 8th Ave. and 1st St. W. It was a famous hostelry for years, having many famous people as guests. It still stands, though now occupied by stores and offices.

The sandstone was quarried locally and was used to build most of Calgary's earlier business blocks.

Calgary's first fire brigade (buckets and ladders) was formed in 1885. Two years later the first fire hall was built on the site of the present Canadian Legion premises. Horse-drawn chemical and pumping engines were purchased and the firemen were all volunteers, rushing from their jobs or from their homes when the alarm bell sounded from the fire hall tower.

In 1908 the volunteer system was replaced by one employing full-time, professional fire fighters. As can well be imagined, Calgary throughout its early history had many notable fires at a time when construction was anything but fireproof and fire fighting equipment was not very effective.

At first, policing was done by the Mounted Police, whose effective presence kept the new frontier town from ever becoming the wild and disorderly place various centres on the Western frontier of the U.S. were said to be.

Municipal police were required as the town grew, however. Prior to 1886 Jack Campbell was town constable and in that year he was succeeded by a force of three men, Jack Ingraham as chief of police and Bob Barton and Bob Barker his two constables. Ingraham was succeeded by Tom Dillabaugh who was followed by Tom English. He commanded a force of 26 constables. In 1909 English was succeeded by Chief Thomas Mackie who raised the force

strength to 43 constables, three sergeants, an inspector and five detectives.

In 1888 a bridge was built across the Bow at Fourth St. E. In 1890 HRH the Duke of Connaught was an important visitor. He turned the first sod on the Calgary to Edmonton railway which was completed in 1891.

A bridge over the Elbow was constructed in 1897 at a cost of $1,240.

Calgary's early pioneers settled east of the Elbow, across the river from the NWMP fort. To their chagrin the CPR built its station west of the Elbow, and so the centre of development moved west soon thereafter and East Calgary did not become the hub of activity expected of it.

In 1899 the General Hospital was incorporated and in 1900 the city purchased the waterworks system operated until then by the Calgary Gas and Waterworks Company.

In 1901 famous visitors to Calgary were the Duke and Duchess of Cornwall and York.

Calgary's first school was conducted by J. W. Costello in Boynton Hall, a log structure located on the site of the Variety Theatre in 1883. Some 10 pupils were enrolled on a fee basis. In 1885 a school district was organized and classes were begun in a frame building located on 9th Ave. E.

Roman Catholic nuns came to the city in March of 1885 and opened separate school classes in a wooden building just east of the Sacred Heart convent. A separate school district was established officially in 1890.

Spencer Douglas was hired as the first public school teacher and

G. C. King

he began his duties April 20, 1885 at a salary of $60 a month.

In 1889 a new school was built at a cost of $8,000. The basement of the Presbyterian Church was utilized for additional classroom space and high school tuition got under way in July of 1890. Three public schools were in operation by 1894 — Central, East Ward and South Ward. Manual training and domestic science classes were begun in 1901 and the school board passed a resolution favoring establishment of a university in Calgary.

Haultain school grounds was the site of the first stone school, a two-room bungalow school being erected there in 1892. Central High School was built in 1908 and added to in 1911. It was Calgary's first high school building. The original Central school was Calgary's first permanent school building. It was built on the site of the present James Short school on 4th Ave. and 1st St. W. The present James Short school was built there in 1904 and named after Calgary's first high school teacher.

Names instead of numbers were used for Calgary streets in the early days. Ninth Ave. was Atlantic Ave. Today's 8th Ave. was called Stephen Avenue in honor of Lord Mount Stephen, CPR president. Seventh Ave. was McIntyre Ave. and 10th Ave. was called Pacific Ave. Seventeenth Ave. was named Notre Dame Ave.

Centre St. was called McTavish St., 1st St. W. was Scarth and 2nd St. W. was Hamilton St. The street running past the town hall and police station (2nd St. E.) was rather inappropriately called Drinkwater St. And the wagon roads to Macleod and Edmonton leading into the city were the Macleod Trail and the Edmonton Trail, names which no longer quite fit the super-highways that would have ruined the hooves of oxen and horses.

In this brief record on Calgary only some of the highlights of its history can be sketched in lightly. But the Calgary Municipal Railway is deserving of mention. On July 2, 1909, two bright, new street cars were unloaded from a

Princess Patricia at the first Calgary Stampede in 1912.

CPR freight car. Three days later they made their first runs as the opening day feature of the Calgary Fair. The city with a population of 35,000 now had the beginning of an electric street railway system which grew and flourished, though it had a habit of returning deficits on occasion.

In 1946 it was decided to convert from rail to bus transportation and the old Calgary Municipal Railway which had kept the city in the forefront of modernity for so long, was replaced by the new Calgary Transit System with its trolley and diesel buses travelling on rubber tires. The last street car made its final run in 1950. Citizens whose memories go back 20 or 30 years will never forget the swaying, clanking runs down Centre St. and 14th St. W.. hills. Some even can remember back to the early Twenties when a ponderous looking sight-seeing car was one of the city's tourist attractions.

The First World War ended the "cowtown" pioneer era for Calgary. After that came the changes of the Twenties and the Thirties, culminating in the Great Depression and a Second World War. Once again Calgary's character changed.

Since the last world war the city has quadrupled in size, its growth being hastened by the surging growth of Alberta's petroleum industry. Where, prior to 1939, you could walk down the street and through the stores and run into familiar faces and figures at almost every turn, now Calgary has become more of a metropolis with an impersonal air, with people rushing about looking pre-occupied and busy and with streets choked with motorized traffic.

The spreading suburbs, with their neat, modern homes, and the big office and apartment buildings which have sprung up one after the other in recent years, have altered the city's appearance. But the Calgary character remains something unique in Canada. It still retains a flavor of the old ranching days, intermingled with a touch of free-wheeling Americanism and a spirit of individual enterprise and imagination.

The Calgary Stampede, born in 1912, has helped consolidate the old tradition and is known the world over. And it was the Calgary spirit generated by the first and only win of the Grey Cup by our Calgary Stampeders in 1948 that turned that annual sports special into a national East-West classic.

Favored by climate and location near the world's greatest mountain wonderland, Calgary also has been blessed by men whose success in business has been matched by their sense of public responsibility. The Glenbow Foundation, Heritage Park, McMahon Stadium, the aquarium, museum collections, scholarships and other memorials have helped enrich the civic heritage.

Col. James Walker

95

First envisioned in 1905, the University of Calgary became a fact April 15, 1966, after a branch of the University of Alberta was established at the Southern Alberta Institute of Technology in 1945. First sod for the university site was turned in 1958, almost 50 years after pioneer Calgarians had set aside another tract of land for the long-delayed dream.

It has been The Calgary Herald's privilege to have been associated with this city's history since 1883 soon after its start as a settlement, and to have recorded that history from day to day. This written record is maintained on microfilm and provides an ever-ready source of material for researchers wishing to delve into the past.

Calgary can boast a richly interesting period of growth from infanthood to maturity. If the courage and vision which created it are maintained by succeeding generations, it is bound to have an enviable future.

The University of Calgary: A - engineering complex, phase 3; B - Students' Union building site; 1 - arts and education; 2 and 2A - science; 3 - physical education; 4 - library; 5 - engineering; 6 - Calgary Hall; 7 - dormitories; 8 - dining centre; 9 - theatre.

This is part of the first Calgary settlement, east of the Elbow River, showing the C.P.R. tracks (in centre); about 1883.

The Edmonton stage, leaving Calgary about 1890.

Downtown Calgary, looking southwest . . . booming . . .

Photo By Michael Burn, Herald Photographer

. . . and prosperous.

Today's Calgary: a metropolis covering 155 square miles
(the biggest Canadian city in area under one municipal

Photo By Michael Burn, Herald Photographer
government), with a population of 335,000 persons.

PICTURES

LITHOGRAPHED IN CANADA
BY

CANNIFF PRINTING
(1964) LTD.
CALGARY, ALBERTA
DECEMBER, 1966